The Smart MSME

Scale Smart. Get IPO Ready.

Structure Your Business. Scale Smart.
Go Public with Confidence.

CA B M AGGARWAL
ABHISHEK AGGARWAL

B M Aggarwal

The Smart MSME

Scale Smart. Get IPO Ready.

Imprint: Independently Published
Cover Design: Canva Pro
Official Website: www.bmaggarwal.com

Disclaimer

The information provided in this book, *The Smart MSME: Scale Smart. Get IPO Ready*, is for general educational and informational purposes only. While every effort has been made to ensure accuracy and reliability, the author and publisher make no representations or warranties regarding the completeness, accuracy, applicability, or suitability of the content contained herein.

This book is **not intended to serve as legal, financial, accounting, or investment advice**. Readers are strongly advised to consult with qualified professionals and regulatory authorities — before making any business, investment, or strategic decisions based on the material in this book.

Any examples, tools, case studies, or strategies mentioned are illustrative and should not be construed as guarantees of future results or business performance. The author and publisher expressly disclaim any liability, loss, or risk incurred — directly or indirectly — as a result of the application of any information contained in this book.

This publication is the intellectual property of the author. No part of this book may be reproduced, stored, or transmitted in any form or by any means — electronic, mechanical, photocopying, recording, scanning, or otherwise — without the prior written permission of the author, except in the case of brief quotations used in critical reviews or articles.

All brand names, trademarks, and company names mentioned are the property of their respective owners, and are used here for reference purposes only.

All disputes, if any, are subject to the jurisdiction of courts in **Delhi, India** only.

Foreword

By Mr. Vijay Bansal
Chairman & Managing Director,
Cantabil Retail India Ltd.

I've always believed that real transformation in business comes not just from vision — but from the right strategy, systems, and partners. When Cantabil Retail India Ltd. decided to go public over a decade ago, it was a major turning point for us. We weren't just raising capital but stepping into a new league of accountability, ambition, and institutional scale.

Like many Indian SMEs, we didn't have a roadmap. That's where CA B. M. Aggarwal entered our journey—not just as a Chartered Accountant but also as a trusted guide, strategist, and IPO architect.

Under his leadership and deep financial expertise, Cantabil raised ₹105 crore through its IPO in 2010 — a landmark success. But his contribution didn't end there. The systems, strategic clarity, and investor-readiness he helped us build back then laid the foundation for the business we've become today.

From a successful IPO to achieving a turnover of ₹721 crore and a PAT of ₹75crore, Cantabil's journey has been one of scale, resilience, and constant evolution. I can say with confidence that the seeds of this transformation were sown with the right IPO preparation, handled by the right mentor.

That's why I believe this book is both timely and necessary.

The Smart MSME is not just another book on business growth. It's a field-tested, founder-focused guide for entrepreneurs who are serious about taking their MSME to the next level—not just through effort but also through strategy, structure, and scale readiness.

B. M. Aggarwal's style has always been no-nonsense, practical, precise, and rooted in decades of hands-on experience. In these pages, he's shared what most consultants never do: the actual systems and tools that help businesses plug growth leaks, attract premium clients, build empowered teams, and yes — even prepare for public listing.

If you are an MSME founder who feels stuck, overwhelmed, or unsure how to grow beyond survival, this book is your wake-up call. It doesn't promise shortcuts. It promises clarity. And in business, that's often the most valuable asset.

I wholeheartedly recommend this book to every serious entrepreneur who wants to stop firefighting and start scaling — with purpose, precision, and peace of mind.

Vijay Bansal
Chairman & Managing Director
Cantabil Retail India Limited

Foreword

By Dr. Amit Maheshwari
CEO - Mettas Overseas Limited
India Head - Kaibex Elevator Tx USA
International Business Trainer &
Motivational Speaker

In my years of training, mentoring, and speaking to thousands of entrepreneurs across India and abroad, I've noticed one truth that rarely gets spoken aloud:

Most MSMEs don't fail due to lack of effort. They fail due to lack of structure.

Indian business owners are among the most hardworking and passionate in the world. But what holds them back is not ambition — it's that no one taught them how to build a business that can grow without breaking them.

That's why this book, The Smart MSME, is so relevant and so powerful.

I've known CA B. M. Aggarwal not just as a seasoned Chartered Accountant, but as a mission-driven mentor who genuinely cares about the growth and dignity of MSME founders. He brings with him over 46 years of rich, hands-on experience — not in theory, but in real-world impact: conducting IPOs, building systems, and guiding founders through the journey from survival to scale.

This book is the culmination of that lifetime of insight. It doesn't talk down to the reader. It meets them where they are.

whether they're stuck in daily chaos, struggling with inconsistent sales, or unsure how to attract the right team, clients, or investors. And it offers clear, step-by-step systems that MSMEs can apply — even if they're not tech-savvy or VC-funded.

What I particularly appreciate is that this is not a motivational book. It's not filled with buzzwords or complex frameworks.

It's filled with real business wisdom — the kind that simplifies, clarifies, and makes founders say, "Yes, this I can do."

From positioning and pricing, to team management and dashboards, to IPO-readiness and investor storytelling — The Smart MSME is the playbook we've been missing in India.

If you're an MSME founder who wants to scale with confidence, stand out in a crowded market, and build a business that doesn't just pay the bills but builds a legacy — read this book.

And more importantly, use this book. Because MSMEs are not small businesses. They are the largest force of employment, innovation, and wealth creation in this country. But they will only thrive if we give them the tools, the systems, and the confidence to lead.

B. M. Aggarwal has given them just that.

Dr. Amit Maheshwari
CEO - Mettas Overseas Limited
India Head - Kaibex Elevator Tx USA
International Business Trainer & Motivational Speaker
Business Mentor | Educator

Preface

If you're holding this book, you're probably not new to the business world — and you're certainly not new to hard work.

You've built something from the ground up. You've taken risks, made sacrifices, and faced sleepless nights over payroll, pricing, production, and people. You've figured things out without a rulebook, survived market chaos, and kept your doors open even when the odds were stacked against you.

But deep down, you also know something else: **Hard work alone is no longer enough.**

I've seen this story play out across India in thousands of MSMEs over the last four decades. I've seen brilliant founders struggle with growth, not because they lacked vision — but because they lacked **structure**. Not because they were lazy — but because they were **stuck in the day-to-day.**

Somewhere between starting up and scaling up, they became the bottleneck.

They couldn't delegate, so they became the answer to every problem.

They couldn't systemise, so their growth became erratic and exhausting.

They couldn't differentiate, so they ended up in price wars. And eventually, many gave up the dream of building something big — just because they didn't have the right map.

That's why I wrote *The Smart MSME.*

This book is not a collection of ideas. It's a **blueprint born from the field** — forged over 46+ years of advising, mentoring, and building with real founders like you.

I've worked with MSMEs across industries — from manufacturing to IT, textiles to services. I've published financial periodicals, led IPOs worth hundreds of crores as a sole advisor, and coached thousands of business owners who felt the same frustration you're probably feeling right now.

And through it all, one insight became crystal clear:

You don't have to hustle harder. You need to scale smarter.

MSMEs aren't failing because of competition. They're failing because of commoditisation. They aren't stuck due to lack of effort. They're stuck due to lack of clarity, systems, and strategy.

This book gives you all three.

The Smart MSME is divided into clear, actionable chapters that walk you step-by-step through:

- Diagnosing your real growth blockers
- Building a "category of one" positioning
- Crafting irresistible offers
- Creating a consistent flow of leads
- Fixing your sales engine
- Installing systems, dashboards, and team clarity
- Building a business that can run — and grow — without your daily control
- And if you're ready, preparing for institutional growth or an IPO

Each chapter is filled with practical tools, real-world examples, and systems that you can start applying immediately. This is not theory. This is what has worked in the trenches — with real Indian businesses that went from chaos to clarity, from stuck to scalable, and in some cases, from local to listed.

But beyond tools and templates, this book is a mindset shift.

It's about helping you move from being a busy operator... To becoming a peaceful, powerful, and prepared business owner.

So as you read this book, don't just skim. Reflect. Take notes. Revisit chapters. Discuss them with your team. Run internal sessions. Use the dashboards, frameworks, and checklists. Implement slowly, but consistently.

Because here's what I truly believe:

MSMEs are not small businesses. They are the backbone of India. And with the right systems and support, they can become the **face of India's future.**

This book is my small contribution toward that vision — and my invitation to you to build not just a business, but a legacy.

Let's get started.

CA B. M. Aggarwal
Chartered Accountant | MSME Mentor | IPO Strategist
Founder – MSME Growth Circle
www.bmaggarwal.com

Acknowledgements

I extend my heartfelt gratitude to everyone who played a role in shaping and supporting the creation of this book, *The Smart MSME: Scale Smart. Get IPO Ready*.

First and foremost, I thank the countless MSME founders who have shared their experiences, challenges, and insights with me over the years. Your journeys — filled with grit, ambition, and resilience — have been the true inspiration behind this book. Your voices and realities are what make this work authentic, practical, and grounded.

I'm also deeply grateful to the professionals and institutions who've supported India's SME ecosystem — including regulatory bodies, merchant bankers, financial advisors, and compliance experts. Your perspectives have contributed to the depth and accuracy of the ideas presented here.

A very special mention must go to **Mr. Abhishek Aggarwal**, whose dedication, insights, and writing contributions have been invaluable throughout this journey. His strategic thinking and commitment to clarity rightfully earn him the title of **Co-Author** of this book.

To my family and close friends — thank you for your unwavering support, patience, and encouragement during the writing and revision process. Your belief in my mission means more than words can express.

Finally, I sincerely thank the editorial team and publishing partners who worked behind the scenes to ensure this manuscript came to life with precision and professionalism.

To all who contributed, directly or indirectly — I am deeply grateful.

Introduction to the Author

CA B M Aggarwal

Chartered Accountant | MSME Mentor | IPO Strategist | Author | Founder – MSME Growth Circle

CA B. M. Aggarwal is one of India's most respected voices in the MSME and financial consulting ecosystem, with an extraordinary track record of over **46 years** across financial strategy, business transformation, and capital markets.

A **Chartered Accountant by qualification and a business mentor by mission**, he has seamlessly transitioned from publishing financial periodicals to mentoring founders, from executing IPOs with finesse to building growth systems that empower MSMEs to operate at scale.

India's Trusted IPO Advisor

CA Aggarwal has built an enviable legacy in the domain of **SME IPO consulting**, having advised and led the successful listing of multiple companies with **public issues worth hundreds of crores**. Known for his clarity, compliance expertise, and founder-friendly guidance, he's often the **sole advisor** behind many high-impact listings. His approach —

sharp, ethical, and system-driven — makes him a go-to name for any SME serious about going public.

Championing India's MSMEs

Having worked closely with entrepreneurs across sectors, he understands the everyday operational chaos MSMEs face — juggling finance, fire-fighting, and fragmented growth. In response, he founded The MSME Growth Circle, a trusted mentorship community designed to help **100,000+ Indian SMEs** build structured, systemised, and standout businesses — without depending on price cuts or guesswork.

His mentoring philosophy is grounded in one powerful promise:

"No Gyaan. No Fluff. Just real, actionable business systems that work."

Author, Educator & Thought Leader

As an educator and author, CA Aggarwal combines deep financial expertise with clear business logic. He has authored two widely respected titles:

Indian SMEs & The Power of SME IPO – a practical playbook to demystify India's SME listing ecosystem and unlock valuation

Pitch Like a Pro – a strategic guide to fundraising, pitch decks, and investor storytelling for startup and SME founders

With his third and most comprehensive book, **The Smart MSME: Scale Smart. Get IPO Ready**, he now offers a **complete blueprint** to help founders move from daily chaos to an IPO-ready business — using structure, systems, and strategic thinking.

Contact Mr. Aggarwal
Website: https://bmaggarwal.com
Email: ipocare@gmail.com
LinkedIn: https://www.linkedin.com/in/bmaggarwal/
Instagram: https://www.instagram.com/cabmaggarwal/
YouTube: https://www.youtube.com/@BMAggarwal

Disclaimer

The information provided in this book, *The Smart MSME: Scale Smart. Get IPO Ready*, is for general educational and informational purposes only. While every effort has been made to ensure accuracy and reliability, the author and publisher make no representations or warranties regarding the completeness, accuracy, applicability, or suitability of the content contained herein.

This book is **not intended to serve as legal, financial, accounting, or investment advice**. Readers are strongly advised to consult with qualified professionals and regulatory authorities — before making any business, investment, or strategic decisions based on the material in this book.

Any examples, tools, case studies, or strategies mentioned are illustrative and should not be construed as guarantees of future results or business performance. The author and publisher expressly disclaim any liability, loss, or risk incurred — directly or indirectly — as a result of the application of any information contained in this book.

This publication is the intellectual property of the author. No part of this book may be reproduced, stored, or transmitted in any form or by any means — electronic, mechanical, photocopying, recording, scanning, or otherwise — without the prior written permission of the author, except in the case of brief quotations used in critical reviews or articles.

All brand names, trademarks, and company names mentioned are the property of their respective owners, and are used here for reference purposes only. All disputes, if any, are subject to the jurisdiction of courts in **Delhi, India** only.

Table of Contents

Chapter 1: The Dream of Going Public

Why MSMEs Should Aim for the Stock Exchange Listing

Let's be brutally honest for a second.

Most MSME owners start their business with passion... but not a plan.

The vision? Fuzzy.

The goals? Shifting every quarter.

The growth strategy? Non-existent or stuck inside someone's head.

And then what happens? Business becomes a day-to-day survival game: firefighting, juggling, and responding to problems. There's no *real* control over direction.

If you've ever felt like that — like you're just moving but not really moving forward — then *this chapter is your wake-up call.*

Because here's the truth:

"Businesses don't fail due to lack of effort. They fail due to lack of direction."

And that's exactly why we're starting this book with a foundational but often neglected piece: **your growth strategy.**

The Invisible Trap: Drifting Without a Vision

Let me ask you something: Can you describe your business vision in one clear sentence?

Most MSMEs can't.

And it's not because they're incapable— they've never paused long enough to define it.

Without a clear vision, even good businesses do **too many things for too many people** — becoming everything to everyone and standing out to no one.

I once met a manufacturing entrepreneur in Pune who proudly told me, "We do everything — whatever the client asks, we'll make it."

He was doing okay — but he was exhausted, his team was confused, and his profit margins were a joke.

Why? No clear vision. No clear direction.

The first section of this chapter will help you **cut through the noise and define your business vision** — not just what you do, but who you are, who you serve, and where you're heading. Because without that, every decision becomes a guess.

Why Growth Goals Without a System Fail

Now, even if you have a vague idea of where you want to go, that's not enough.

Vision is your destination. But what about the journey?

That's where goal-setting comes in. But not the "Let's double our revenue this year!" kind of goal-setting. Clear, measurable, time-bound goals that drive behaviour and results are **clear, measurable, time-bound goals** that actually drive behaviour and results.

Here's the thing:

"What doesn't get measured doesn't get managed. And what doesn't get managed... slips."

So many MSMEs fall into the trap of chasing "growth" without defining what success looks like.

In the second section of this chapter, we'll break down how to set goals that create momentum — not pressure. Goals that are tied to your unique vision, your team's capacity, and your market realities.

The Scaling Roadmap You've Been Missing

Ever feel like you're stuck in limbo?

You're doing well — but not *that* well.

You're growing — but it's slow, scattered, or painfully unpredictable.

That's often because there's **no roadmap.** Just random decisions, gut instincts, and wishful thinking.

One MSME owner from Gujarat told me, "We're growing... I think. But we don't know what the next step should be."

That's a dangerous place — especially if you want to become IPO-ready. Investors don't put money into "we'll figure it out." They invest in clarity.

In the third part of this chapter, we'll show you how to build a **step-by-step roadmap** that turns your growth goals into milestones and phases. Whether in Stages 1, 2, or 3, you'll see how to map the path ahead and scale without chaos.

Align Your Resources with Right Targets

You now have a solid vision, clear goals, and a roadmap. You're pumped.

But here comes the next trap: **misaligned execution.**

This is where many MSMEs leak time, money, and energy.

They hire a marketing agency without knowing their real USP.

They invest in software without fixing their processes.

They run sales campaigns without training their team.

In short, their **resources and strategy are playing different games.**

In this chapter's fourth and final sub-section, we'll show you how to **align your team, budget, and systems with your actual growth priorities.** You'll learn how to plug resource leaks, delegate smartly, and stay laser-focused on what moves the needle.

What's Waiting Ahead in This Chapter...

This chapter is not just about theory — it's about building **your personalised growth engine**.

By the time you finish it, you'll have:

- A crystal-clear business vision that acts like your North Star
- Tangible growth goals that drive day-to-day actions
- A custom roadmap to scale smartly
- And a strategy to channel your resources without wastage

Clarity creates confidence. Confidence attracts capital. Capital drives IPO-readiness.

So take a deep breath, flip the page, and start where all great businesses begin — with a powerful, purposeful growth strategy.

Start with the End in Mind:

Your Business Vision Matters More Than You Think

Have you ever set out on a road trip without knowing the destination?

You just start the car, drive for hours, stop at dhabas, take turns based on mood—and hope you'll "figure it out" on the way. Sounds fun for a holiday, right?

But imagine doing that with your *business*.

Unfortunately, that's what most MSMEs do. They get into business, start running, and hustle every day—but without clearly defining their goals.

Without a clear vision, even the most passionate entrepreneurs can get stuck in circles. Busy? Yes. Growing? Maybe. Going somewhere meaningful? Hmm... not really.

"A business without a vision is like a ship without a compass. It floats but rarely reaches anywhere worthwhile."

The Foggy Middle: Where Most MSMEs Get Lost

In my 47 years of working with Indian MSMEs, I've noticed a common pattern—especially among businesses that have been around for a few years.

They're doing okay. Cash is flowing (most of the time), customers are coming in, and staff is showing up. On paper, everything looks... fine.

But scratch the surface, and you'll hear things like:

- "We don't know if we're growing in the right direction."
- "Every new year, we try something different."
- "We're always reacting—never really planning."

And here's the dangerous part: They don't even realize they're stuck.

They're moving, yes. But without momentum. And definitely without a magnetic pull toward something bigger.

What a Real Vision Sounds Like

Let's be clear—vision isn't just a motivational quote on your office wall. It's not some fancy paragraph your consultant wrote during a weekend retreat.

A real business vision is a **clear mental picture of success for you**—3, 5, or 10 years from now. It reflects your values, impact, and the life you want to build through your business.

It answers questions like:

- What kind of business do you want to become?
- Who do you want to serve?
- What do you want to be known for in your industry?
- How do you want your team, customers, and partners to feel about working with you?

It's okay if you don't have perfect answers yet. But it's not okay to ignore the questions altogether.

Why Vision Comes First — Always

You might wonder, "Isn't this vision stuff for big companies with MBAs and boardrooms?"

No. It's actually more important for MSMEs.

Because in small businesses, *every decision counts*. You don't have the luxury of trial and error forever. Your money, time, and team are limited. If you don't aim them toward a defined target, you'll waste years and lakhs going in circles.

"Clarity in vision leads to clarity in decision."

Vision isn't just for inspiration; it's for alignment. It becomes the filter through which you say YES or NO to new ideas, clients, team hires, expansions, and even IPO timing.

How to Define Your Vision (Without Corporate Jargon)

Let's make this simple. Here's a quick thought exercise. Take a moment and answer these prompts in your notebook:

1. **In 5 years, my business will be known for...**
2. **The kind of clients I love working with are...**
3. **The impact I want to create is...**
4. **I want my business to help me live a life where I can...**

Don't overthink. Don't make it perfect. Just write what comes naturally. This is not for show. This is your *truth*.

Data shows that businesses with a documented vision are 2X more likely to grow revenue consistently over 5 years.

— [Source: Deloitte MSME Growth Report]

A Three-Part Framework to Articulate Your Vision

If you want to take it a step further, use this simple 3-part framework to define your business vision in a single sentence:

[What you do] + [For whom] + [The impact you want to create]

Examples:

- "We manufacture eco-friendly packaging for FMCG brands that care about sustainability."
- "We provide cloud-based accounting solutions for small retailers so they can manage finances without hiring a CA."
- "We help rural entrepreneurs set up solar microgrids so their villages can get reliable power."

See how clear that is?

Now, imagine making every decision in your business based on this sentence. That's the power of a sharp vision.

Quick Quiz: Is Your Vision Clear?

☑ Can every team member describe your business vision in one line?

☑ Do your products, pricing, and marketing reflect your long-term vision?

☑ Do you use your vision to make daily decisions?

If you answered "No" to any of the above—it's time to revisit and realign.

Before You Move Ahead...

You might be tempted to jump straight into setting goals or scaling tactics.

But slow down.

Without a vision, your goals will lack direction, your team will lack motivation, and your IPO dreams will remain distant.

This chapter started with a quote: "Start with the end in mind."

That's not just advice. That's survival.

Now that you've laid the foundation, let's move to the next layer—**setting Clear Goals for Growth**—and build a plan that's rooted in clarity, not chaos.

Ready? Let's go from vague ambition to laser-sharp action in the next section.

Goals That Move the Needle:

Turning Vision into Action

So, you've defined your business vision. You now know where you want to go. Great!

But let me ask you something.

Do you know *how* you're going to get there?

More importantly — do you know *if* you're making progress?

This is where most MSMEs slip.

Because having a vision is inspiring, but *without clear, trackable goals*, that vision stays locked in your diary — or worse, buried under daily distractions and emergencies.

"Vision without goals is just wishful thinking."

And wishful thinking won't prepare your business for IPO. Concrete goals will.

The Big Lie: "Let's Just Grow Revenue"

I've met hundreds of MSME owners who proudly say, "Our goal this year is to double revenue!"

Sounds exciting.

But here's the problem — it's vague. And vague goals are dangerous.

- Double from what number?
- By when?

- With what resources?
- Through which channel?
- And most importantly... *why?*

"We want to grow" is not a goal. It's a desire.

A real business goal is **specific, measurable, time-bound, and aligned with your bigger strategy**.

The Power of SMART Goals (Yes, They Actually Work)

You've probably heard the term **SMART goals** before. But let's not just quote it — let's understand how it applies to your business right now.

Here's what SMART stands for:

- **Specific** – What exactly do you want to achieve?
- **Measurable** – How will you track progress?
- **Achievable** – Is it realistic based on your resources?
- **Relevant** – Does it align with your vision and strategy?
- **Time-bound** – What's the deadline?

Let's apply this:

Instead of:

"We want to increase our Instagram presence."

Say: *"We want to grow our Instagram follower base by 30% in the next 90 days by posting 3 value-driven reels per week and engaging with 10 potential customers daily."*

Now, *that's* a goal you can track, manage, and hit.

> **"Companies that set clear goals are 376% more likely to report successful outcomes."**
>
> — [Source: Harvard Business Review, SME Performance Study]

Four Types of Goals Every MSME Must Set

Regarding goal setting for IPO-ready growth, you must think beyond sales targets. Here are four core types of goals every MSME should define:

1. Financial Goals

Revenue, profit margin, cost efficiency, debt reduction, cash flow targets — these are the numbers that define your financial fitness.

2. Customer Goals

Customer acquisition, retention, satisfaction scores, referral rates—if you want to attract investors, you must demonstrate customer loyalty and stability.

3. Operational Goals

Turnaround time, production efficiency, error reduction, and system implementation — this is where scalability is built.

4. Team & Culture Goals

Hiring milestones, training hours, employee engagement, retention rates — IPOs are driven by people just as much as products.

Start small. But set one goal in each area — and review them monthly.

Goal vs Growth Trap: Don't Chase Metrics That Don't Matter

Sometimes, we chase numbers that feel good but don't really help.

Likes. Impressions. Vanity revenue without profitability. Product launches with no retention.

Stop. Every goal should pass this test: *"Will achieving this move us closer to our vision and IPO readiness?"* If not, ditch it.

What If You Miss a Goal?

Most people won't tell you *that missing a goal isn't a failure.*

It's feedback.

Sometimes, your assumptions were wrong, the market changed, or you overestimated your capacity. That's okay.

What matters is this:

- Did you track the goal?
- Did you learn from it?
- Did you improve the next one?

Progress is not always a straight line. But it has to be intentional.

Let's Make This Real: Reflect Before You Move Ahead

Take 10 minutes to answer these prompts:

- What is one financial goal I want to achieve in the next 90 days?
- What customer goal will support that?
- What operational habit will make it possible?
- What team behaviour needs to shift to support it?

Write it down. Share it with your team. Make it visible.

"When goals are clear, confusion disappears. Energy gets focused. Results follow."

Now that you've clarified your growth direction and locked in meaningful goals, it's time to create the **roadmap** that will carry you there — step-by-step, stage-by-stage.

Ready to move from isolated goals to a powerful scaling strategy?

Let's dive into the next section: **Creating a Roadmap for Scaling**.

Your Growth Roadmap: Stop Guessing, Start Scaling

Okay, now you've got a clear vision and some solid growth goals.

Great.

But let me ask you something uncomfortable: *Do you know the exact path from where you are... to where you want to go?*

Because most MSMEs don't.

They have ambition and even targets, but they lack one key ingredient—**a roadmap.**

"Without a roadmap, goals become guesswork."

And guesswork is not a strategy. Especially not when you're aiming for an IPO.

The Silent Killer of Scaling: Unstructured Growth

Most MSMEs don't fail because they're lazy. They fail because they're lost in the middle.

Not at the start. Not at the end. But somewhere in between.

This is the danger zone — where you've grown past the initial hustle but haven't yet built a scalable system. So what happens?

- Orders increase, but systems don't.
- The team grows, but communication breaks.
- Clients come in, but delivery quality dips.

It becomes chaos masked as growth.

The Truth About Scaling: It Happens in Stages

Let's bust a myth right now — **growth is not linear.**

It doesn't go: ₹1 crore → ₹2 crore → ₹5 crore → IPO.

There are stages. And each stage has its challenges, rules, and bottlenecks.

Here's a simplified version of what I've observed across hundreds of businesses:

Stage 1: Startup Survival

Focus: Getting clients, proving your model

Challenge: Limited resources, founder doing everything

Stage 2: Stability & Delivery

Focus: Creating consistent service or product delivery

Challenge: Hiring the first team, creating SOPs

Stage 3: Scaling Operations

Focus: Expanding reach and increasing revenue

Challenge: Delegation, quality control, tech adoption

Stage 4: Structured Growth

Focus: Systems, dashboards, leadership team

Challenge: Culture, KPIs, managing cash flow

Stage 5: IPO Readiness

Focus: Financial controls, audit trail, investor pitch

Challenge: Governance, brand authority, valuation

Now, here's the kicker — *you can't skip a stage.*

Jumping from Stage 2 to Stage 5 is like building the third floor before the foundation.

"65% of high-potential MSMEs hit a plateau because they scaled without structure."

— [Source: CII-SME India Growth Survey, 2022]

Build Your Roadmap: A Simple, Repeatable Framework

How do you create a roadmap that doesn't live in theory but actually guides your actions?

Try this 5-step framework:

1. Assess Your Current Stage

Be brutally honest. Are you ready to scale? Or do you still have survival fires burning?

2.   Identify the Next Logical Milestone

Don't jump 10 steps ahead. Pick the next big thing that truly matters—maybe it's hiring a COO, automating billing, or entering a new city.

3.   Break It into Projects

If your milestone is "Expand to Mumbai," then your projects could include market research, finding a warehouse, hiring a local team, and launching a promo campaign.

4.   **Assign Timelines and Owners**

Every project needs a name and a deadline. "We'll do it when we can" is not a strategy.

5.   **Review Monthly. Adjust Quarterly.**

Plans change, markets shift, and that's okay. But without review, even the best roadmap becomes useless.

Avoid This Trap: "More Is Not Better"

Another common mistake? Setting 10 priorities at once.

Listen — *growth is not about doing more things*. It's about doing the right things in the right order.

Visualize It: The Growth Ladder Tool

Here's a simple visual model you can sketch in your notebook:

Stage 1 → Stage 2 → Stage 3 → Stage 4 → Stage 5

(Start)   (Stabilize)   (Scale)   (Structure)   (IPO)

Under each stage, write:

- What defines this stage?
- What's your current biggest challenge?
- What does success at this stage look like?

This ladder becomes your custom roadmap. It gives your team clarity and shows potential investors that you're not running on gut feel—you've got a plan.

Quick Reflection: Where Are You Right Now?

Answer these prompts in your journal:

- What stage of growth are we in?
- What must we fix the #1 bottleneck in the next 60 days?
- What's the one milestone that would unlock the next stage?

Write. Reflect. Share with your leadership team.

"Plans are useless, but planning is everything."

— Dwight Eisenhower

Final Thoughts Before We Move On

Roadmaps aren't about predicting the future. They're about creating direction. They help you say *no* to distractions and *yes* to strategic moves.

If you're serious about scaling — and becoming IPO-ready — your roadmap will become your most valuable internal asset.

It's not your pitch deck. Not your website. Not even your product.

When investors come in, they ask, "Where is this business going, and how will it get there?"

Your roadmap is the answer.

Now that we've built your path forward, it's time to **align your people, money, and time with that path.**

In the next section, we'll tackle something that most MSMEs ignore until it's too late — **resource alignment.** Don't miss it.

Where Focus Goes, Growth Flows: Aligning Resources with Strategy

Let's say you now have a crystal-clear vision. You've nailed your goals. You've even mapped out a beautiful roadmap.

But here's the big question: **Are your resources aligned with your plan?**

If your answer is, "Umm... sort of?" we need to talk.

This is the point at which even the most promising MSMEs start slipping.

You've got the destination and the GPS.

But the fuel? The team? The vehicle? The route?

They're all out of sync.

"Strategy without resource alignment is like trying to win a Formula 1 race on a bicycle."

Sounds harsh? Maybe. But it's true.

The Hidden Growth Leak Most MSMEs Ignore

In most MSMEs I've worked with, I see this pattern:

- Marketing targets one type of client, while the operations team is built for another.
- The founder is chasing 10 ideas, while the team still struggles with the last one.
- Budgets are spent where the noise is — not where the needle moves.

Result? Exhaustion. Missed deadlines. Low ROI. And team burnout. Not because people aren't working hard. But because they're working **in different directions.**

What "Alignment" Actually Means

Let's break this down.

Alignment means your **people, time, and money** are all flowing toward your **primary strategic goals.**

It means saying:

- "No" to opportunities that don't fit your long-term vision
- "Not now" to distractions that pull you sideways
- "Double down" on the things that actually create momentum

In real terms, alignment looks like this:

- Your team knows the quarterly focus — and so do their to-do lists
- Your marketing reflects your current capacity and future positioning
- Your budget prioritizes what's strategic, not just urgent

"Only 29% of Indian MSMEs report that their daily operations are strongly aligned with long-term goals."

— [Source: FICCI-Nasscom MSME Pulse Report, 2023]

Start with People: Team Alignment Is Everything

Your strategy is only as strong as your execution. And your execution is only as good as your team's clarity.

Here's a quick test:

Ask any 5 team members — "What are our top 3 goals this quarter?"

If you get five different answers, that's a red flag.

Here's how to fix it:

- **Monthly team huddles**: Share progress, blockers, and upcoming focus.
- **Clear roles with outcomes**: Every team member should own specific targets.
- **Vision reminders**: Include the company's growth vision in onboarding, training, and weekly emails.

People don't resist strategy. They resist confusion.

The Resource Filter: Where Should You Invest?

You've only got so much time, money, and attention.

So, use this **Resource Alignment Filter** before any major investment:

1. **Does this support our primary goal this quarter?**
2. **Is this the best way to achieve that goal, or just the most visible one?**
3. **What's the expected ROI — in numbers, time saved, or momentum created?**

If it fails this test — pause it, simplify it, or skip it.

Common Misalignments to Watch For

☑ **Marketing vs Capacity**: Don't promise what your backend can't deliver.

☑ **Hiring vs Goals**: Don't hire based on CVs. Hire based on roadmap needs.

☑ **Time vs Strategy**: Founders often spend hours on low-impact tasks. Protect your calendar like your cash.

☑ **Budget vs Outcomes**: More spending ≠, more growth. Focus on spending that builds systems or brand trust.

Ask These 5 Questions Every Month

1. Are our top 3 priorities clear — and reflected in how we spend our time?

2. Is every major expense connected to a strategic outcome?
3. Is our team clear, motivated, and empowered to execute?
4. Are we saying "yes" to the right things and "no" to the rest?
5. Are we measuring the right numbers to track success?

If you can't confidently answer "Yes" to most of these, it's time to realign.

"Growth doesn't come from doing more. It comes from doing what matters — with full focus."

Now that your resources are in sync with your strategy, you're no longer running in circles.

You're building a business that's focused, resilient and *IPO-worthy*.

But we're not done yet.

Having a plan is one thing; **sticking to it, tracking it, and tweaking it** is a whole different skill.

The next section will explore **measuring progress, handling surprises, and staying on course without losing steam.** Let's move forward.

What Gets Measured, Gets Moved:

Tracking Progress Without Losing Focus

So, you've got your growth strategy.

Your goals are sharp.

Your roadmap is clear.

Your resources are aligned.

But here's the twist — **none of it matters if you're not tracking progress.**

I know. It sounds boring. Numbers, dashboards, reports...

But let me tell you something that decades of experience have taught me:

"Success doesn't come from ambition. It comes from execution. And execution needs accountability."

Without measurement, your vision is just a dream. With measurement, it becomes a plan.

The Execution Gap: Where Great Strategies Die

I've seen brilliant MSMEs create ambitious plans and forget to check if it's working.

They launch marketing campaigns without tracking ROI.

They hire salespeople without setting monthly targets.

They set revenue goals but never compare actuals vs projections.

It's like setting a destination in Google Maps... and driving with your eyes closed.

Why Founders Avoid Tracking (and Why That's Dangerous)

Let's be honest — many MSME founders don't track consistently.

Not because they're lazy.

But because tracking feels...

- Complicated

- Time-consuming

- "Corporate"

And sometimes, painful. Because numbers don't lie; they show you what's broken.

But that's the point.

"The role of a leader isn't to feel good. It's to see clearly."

If you avoid data, you avoid the truth. And the truth is what builds IPO-ready businesses.

Five Things Every MSME Must Track

Let's simplify this. You don't need 100 KPIs and fancy software. Start with these five essentials:

1. Sales Conversion Rate

How many leads become paying clients?

Why it matters: Shows the quality of your sales process, pitch, and follow-up.

2. Customer Retention Rate

How many clients come back to buy again?

Why it matters: IPO investors love stable revenue — not one-time buyers.

3. Monthly Cash Flow

Are you consistently earning more than you spend?

Why it matters: Revenue is vanity. Cash flow is survival.

4. Team Performance Metrics

Are your team members meeting their goals?

Why it matters: You can't scale if only the founder performs.

5. Project Completion Rate

How many of your internal initiatives get finished on time?

Why it matters: Execution is where businesses win or lose.

"High-performing businesses are 42% more likely to review their KPIs weekly."

— [Source: Indian MSME Growth Trends Report, 2023]

Tools That Don't Overwhelm You

You don't need an ERP or fancy CRM to get started. Begin with simple tools like:

- **Google Sheets or Excel**: Make a dashboard tab. Update every Friday.

- **Trello or Asana**: Track project milestones and task ownership.

- **WhatsApp Weekly Updates**: Ask each team lead to share three key numbers every Monday.

- **Simple CRM**: Even a free version (like Zoho or HubSpot) can track leads and conversions.

Consistency matters more than complexity.

Visual Cue: The Weekly Pulse Dashboard

Here's a format you can use to create your snapshot:

Metric	Target	Actual	Owner	Status
Weekly Sales (₹)	₹1,00,000	₹87,000	Rahul	⚠
Follow-ups Done	50	55	Seema	✓
Projects Completed	3	2	Ramesh	⚠
Website Traffic (visits)	2000	2150	Shalini	✓
Cash Flow (Monthly)	₹3L+	₹2.8L	Founder	⚠

Track. Review. Discuss. Improve. Repeat.

How to Stay on Track (Even When You Slip)

Let's get real — things won't always go as planned.

You'll miss targets. A project will fall behind. A new hire won't perform.

That's okay.

Tracking isn't about guilt; it's about **course correction**.

Here's what smart founders do:

1. **Review weekly**: Don't wait till quarter-end to panic.

2. **Identify patterns**: One miss? Ignore. Repeated miss? Investigate.

3. **Make micro-adjustments**: Shift resources, tweak offers, reset timelines.

4. **Celebrate small wins**: Momentum is built by progress, not perfection.

Before You Move On...

Here's a quick reflection exercise. Write down:

*   Which 3 numbers define success for your business right now?
*   How often do you check them?
*   Who else on your team tracks them?

Now schedule a recurring 30-minute "Review Ritual" in your calendar. Make it non-negotiable.

"If you don't measure it, you can't improve it. If you don't improve it, you can't scale it."

Congratulations — you've just completed the full foundation of your **Growth Strategy Engine.**

You've defined your direction, set goals, mapped your journey, aligned your resources, and learned to track everything like a real business leader.

The next major leap comes: **Solving operational bottlenecks and preparing your backend for true scalability.** Growth is great, but only if your systems can handle it.

Chapter 2: Fix the Foundation First

Operational Excellence Before Expansion

Every business wants to scale.

You dream of higher revenue, more customers, wider markets, and maybe even, one day — going public.

But here's the truth that many founders ignore (until it hits them hard):

You can't scale chaos.

And yet, that's exactly what most MSMEs try to do.

They get the marketing going. They start acquiring leads. Orders begin to flow.

And then... everything breaks.

- Orders get delayed.
- Team members get overloaded.
- Customers start complaining.
- You're constantly firefighting.
- And the founder? Drowning in daily decisions.

The growth doesn't feel like a celebration — it feels like a crisis.

Why? Because the **foundation isn't ready**.

This chapter is about fixing that.

It's about strengthening your business's operational engine so it doesn't collapse under the weight of success.

Because if you want to grow fast, you must first become **stable**, **scalable**, and **system-driven**.

Why This Chapter Matters More Than You Think

Marketing gets attention.

Sales get revenue.

But operations? **Operations deliver the promise.**

And if you can't deliver well, no amount of marketing can save you.

Your operations define your **capacity to grow**.

If they're strong, you scale with confidence.

If they're weak, you scale with fear — or worse, you stop scaling altogether.

In this chapter, we'll help you clear the clutter and build a business that's ready for real growth — without breaking. Let's walk through the five parts:

Find the Jam Before You Press the Accelerator: Spotting Operational Bottlenecks

You feel like your team is always busy... but not really productive.

You're working hard... but still missing deadlines.

Chances are, you're stuck in hidden **bottlenecks**.

In this section, we'll help you identify the exact places where things get stuck:

- Tasks that rely on one person
- Processes with unnecessary approvals
- Systems that create friction instead of flow

You'll learn how to map your workflows, spot the blockages, and start fixing them — before they derail your growth.

Smooth Is Fast – Streamline Your Processes Before You Grow

Most MSMEs grow through "jugaad" — patchwork processes that barely hold together.

But when demand spikes, those shortcuts collapse.

This section teaches you how to **simplify, standardize, and systemize** your daily operations.

You'll discover:

- How to turn chaos into clear checklists
- How to build SOPs that your team actually uses
- How to eliminate steps that waste time
- How to create speed without losing quality

Because **streamlined businesses scale faster — and smoother.**

Scale Without Breaking – Build for Tomorrow, Not Just Today

You might be okay today.

But what happens when orders double? When your team expands? When you launch new products?

That's when your **systems and people** are tested.

This section shows you how to **build scalability into your operations** from day one.

You'll learn:

- How to automate the right things
- How to track key metrics before they become blind spots
- How to hire for growth, not just for gaps
- How to create capacity — not just survive demand

If you want to grow without pain, this section is your blueprint.

Your Growth Is Only as Good as Your People – Build a Team That Scales with You

Let's be honest.

Your operations don't run on tools or SOPs. They run on people.

And if your team isn't aligned, trained, or empowered — your systems will fail.

This section helps you:

- Hire for ownership, not just skill
- Delegate with confidence (and clarity)
- Create middle managers who reduce your workload
- Build daily and weekly rhythms that drive accountability

Because your team is either your biggest asset — or your biggest bottleneck.

Handle the Heat – Managing Rising Demand Without Crashing

Growth brings pressure. And pressure exposes weak systems, stressed teams, and poor planning.

This final section is your playbook for **handling sudden growth** without losing your mind.

You'll discover:

- How to create delivery buffers without losing speed
- How to tier your customers for smoother service
- How to automate repeatable tasks to free up human focus
- How to manage team energy and avoid burnout
- How to keep quality high even when demand spikes

Because growth should feel exciting — *not exhausting*.

What You'll Gain from This Chapter

By the end of this chapter, you'll have:

✓ A clear map of your current operational flaws

✓ Systems and SOPs that reduce stress and errors

☑ A team that supports — not slows — your growth

☑ The confidence to scale without fear

☑ A business that's no longer run by chance — but by **choice**

This is the backbone of long-term success.

This is what investors, partners, and customers *really* look for.

And this is what will make your business **IPO-worthy.**

So, let's fix what's under the hood — before we press the accelerator.

Find the Jam Before You Press the Accelerator:

Spotting Operational Bottlenecks

If you've ever wondered why your team is always busy but your output doesn't reflect it… you're not alone.

If your sales are increasing but your profits aren't…

If your customers are happy with your product but frustrated with your service…

If your processes "work" until things get even a little busy, and then everything breaks…

You're likely stuck in the invisible trap of **operational bottlenecks**.

"Growth doesn't break your business. It exposes what's already broken."

If you don't fix these before scaling, trust me, they'll grow with you, multiply, choke your systems, drain your people, and eventually suffocate your momentum.

So… What Exactly Is a Bottleneck?

In simple words — a bottleneck is any **step in your business process that slows everything else down**.

It's the weakest link in the chain. The traffic jam in an otherwise open highway.

Sometimes, it's a system, sometimes a tool, and often, it's a person (yes, including the founder).

And the scariest part? **Most businesses don't know where their bottlenecks actually are.**

Because when things are chaotic, everything feels urgent. But not everything is *important*. Not everything is *the real issue*.

Common Bottlenecks That MSMEs Overlook

Let's break it down. These are the usual suspects:

⧉ Process Bottlenecks

- Too many manual steps
- Lack of documented SOPs
- Tasks getting stuck waiting for approvals

👥 People Bottlenecks

- One person holds too much knowledge (founder syndrome)
- Low delegation, high micromanagement
- Overloaded team members

⚒ Tech Bottlenecks

- Using outdated tools that don't scale
- Lack of integration between systems (CRM, billing, inventory)
- Data scattered across WhatsApp, Excel, Google Drive

✿ Communication Bottlenecks

- There is no central place for task tracking
- Endless follow-up calls and "status update" messages
- Customer queries lost between departments

💰 Financial Bottlenecks

- Delays in invoicing
- Credit terms that slow down cash flow
- Approvals stuck due to unclear authority

Do any of these feel familiar?

You don't need to fix them all today. But identifying them? That's the first win.

"In one study, 73% of SME founders said their business ran smoother when they stepped away for 7 days — because the team had to find and fix hidden bottlenecks."

— [Source: TiE India Report, 2022]

Quick Exercise: Map Your Workflow

Write down one key process in your business—for example, **"Lead to Delivery"** or **"Client Onboarding."**

Literally. Step 1, Step 2, Step 3...

Then ask:

- Where do things get stuck?
- Where do mistakes repeat?
- Who are the frequent blockers?
- How often does this process get delayed or escalated?

Highlight those spots. That's where your bottlenecks live.

Do this for just **one process per week**, and you'll start clearing serious space in your system.

Bottlenecks Are Not Bad News:

Yes, you read that right.

Because once you spot them, you gain an unfair advantage.

They point to exactly where your next level of growth is hiding. They tell you what to fix, who to train, what to automate, or what to stop doing altogether.

They turn your business from reactive to proactive.

"Don't fear bottlenecks. Fear not knowing where they are."

Before You Move On...

Take a few minutes to reflect:

- What's one process in my business that constantly causes stress or delay?
- Is the problem with tools, steps, people, or clarity?
- What's *one small fix* I can try this week?

In the next section, we will **start fixing** those broken parts.

We'll look at how to **streamline operations for speed, reliability, and scale** — without creating chaos.

Ready? Let's roll up our sleeves and simplify the engine.

Smooth Is Fast: Streamline Your Processes Before You Grow

Imagine you're driving a brand-new SUV on a bumpy village road full of potholes.

Now imagine driving the same SUV on a newly paved expressway.

Same vehicle. Same engine. But the second one will take you faster, smoother, and with far less fuel.

That's exactly how streamlined processes work in business.

When your operations are broken, it doesn't matter how great your product is — your growth will always be jerky, slow, and expensive.

But when your backend runs smoothly? Growth becomes predictable. Scalable. And actually *enjoyable*.

"Streamlining isn't about doing more work. It's about doing less — with more impact."

The Real Cost of Clunky Operations

Let's be honest. Most MSMEs are full of "jugaad."

Makeshift processes. Verbal handovers. WhatsApp chaos. One Excel sheet that holds the fate of 10 crores in business.

At first, it feels smart. Agile. "We're saving money!"

But here's what it *actually* costs you:

- Time wasted in follow-ups and confusion

- Errors due to miscommunication
- Angry clients due to late deliveries
- Burned-out team members juggling too much
- Lost opportunities due to poor coordination

And no investor touches a business that runs on band-aids.

Step 1: Map the Madness

You can't simplify what you haven't visualized.

Pick any process — say, "Lead to Order" — and list the exact steps involved. Yes, all of them.

What happens after a lead calls? Who follows up? What gets sent? How is it tracked? What's manual? What's digital? Where are the gaps?

Even if this takes 2 hours, do it. This messy map is the first step to clarity. Now look at this map and ask:

- Which steps can be **eliminated**?
- Which steps can be **automated**?
- Which steps can be **delegated**?
- Which steps are **duplicated or unclear**?

Highlight the leaks. That's where your time and energy are getting sucked.

The 3S Rule: Simplify → Standardize → Systemize

Let's use this golden rule to fix the mess.

✓ 1. Simplify

- Remove unnecessary steps.

- Cancel out double approvals.
- Eliminate "we've always done it this way" steps.

Example: Instead of 5 follow-ups from 3 people, one person calls with a checklist and updates the CRM. Boom — 4 calls saved.

☑ 2. Standardize

- Create a checklist for recurring tasks.
- Use templates for emails, quotes, or reports.
- Decide fixed turnaround times.

Example: All customer complaints are acknowledged within 4 hours — no exception.

☑ 3. Systemize

- Use simple tools to track progress.
- Automate repetitive tasks where possible.
- Keep data in one central place — not scattered.

Example: New leads from your website auto-flow into TeleCRM, trigger an email, and assign a sales rep.

This is not "tech stuff." This is how professional businesses are built.

"Businesses that document and standardize even three core processes see 2X higher operational efficiency."

— [Source: MSME India Efficiency Report, 2023]

Simple Tools to Streamline Operations

You don't need a ₹10 lakh ERP.

Here are affordable tools many of my clients use:

- **Google Sheets** – For tracking orders, leads, tasks
- **TeleCRM** – For lead follow-up, pipeline, auto-reminders
- **Trello / Asana** – For managing daily work across teams
- **Zapier / Integrately** – For automating tasks between apps
- **New Zenler** – For automating training, onboarding, or education-based funnels

Pick one. Start small. The goal is not perfection — it's progress.

Daily Chaos to Daily Clarity: The Magic of SOPs

I know "SOP" sounds like corporate jargon. But let me translate:

SOP = How we do things here, every single time.

It can be:

- A checklist
- A flowchart
- A screen-recorded video
- A written doc with steps and screenshots

The format doesn't matter. **Consistency does.**

Create SOPs for:

- Onboarding a client
- Processing an order
- Escalating a support issue
- Running payroll
- Sending follow-up emails

It saves time. Prevents errors. Builds team confidence. And creates trust when you're delegating.

Quick Reflection: Where Can You Start?

Take a pen and answer these now:

- What's one recurring task that always causes stress?
- What part of your process gets repeated 5 times a week?
- What's one thing you do manually that software could handle?
- What can only *you* do — and what are you still doing that someone else should?

You'll find your starting point right there.

"Your future scalability depends more on your current systems than your current sales."

In the next section, we'll take this further.

Because simplifying is great. But what about **scaling**?

Let's explore the tools, technologies, and methods that will allow your business to grow without breaking because you deserve to scale smart — not suffer in silence.

Scale Without Breaking:

Build for Tomorrow, Not Just Today

Let's say your orders suddenly triple next quarter.

Would your business celebrate... or collapse?

Would your systems absorb the growth — or choke under the pressure?

Would your team rise to the occasion — or burn out in the chaos?

This isn't a hypothetical question. It's a reality that hits many MSMEs the moment their product starts getting attention or when that one big order finally lands.

"If your business isn't built to scale, success will feel like stress."

That's why streamlining is just step one.

The next move? You build for scale.

You shift your mindset from "What's working now?" to "What will still work when we grow 10X?"

The Myth of "We'll Fix It Later"

Here's the trap: Founders often delay system building because "right now we're small."

They say things like:

- "We'll get software once we grow bigger."

- "Let's hire properly after we bag that deal."

- "We'll set up a process later — it's faster if I just do it now."

Sound familiar?

I get it. When you're small, speed feels more important than structure.

But the truth?

The structure is what enables sustainable speed.

Skipping this step is like trying to build the second floor while ignoring cracks in the ground floor.

What Makes a Business Scalable?

Scalability isn't just about handling more orders.

It's about **increasing output without increasing pain.**

Here's what a scalable business typically has:

- **Repeatable processes** (so new people can do the job well)
- **Automation systems** (so you don't need five people to do one person's work)
- **Data tracking** (so you can predict, not guess)
- **Resource flexibility** (so you can scale up without drama)
- **Delegation culture** (so the founder is not the bottleneck)

Let's unpack these and show you how to build each.

1. Document the Repeatable

Start with your most revenue-generating process.

Maybe it's "Inbound Lead to Order Confirmation."

Break it into repeatable steps. Write them down. Record them if needed.

Now ask: *Can someone else follow this tomorrow without asking me 10 questions?*

If yes — you're scalable.

If not — you're still a one-person army.

Start documenting one key process per week. You'll thank yourself in six months.

2. Automate the Repetitive

Let's be clear — automation doesn't mean robots taking over your business.

It means using tools to take care of what doesn't need human brainpower.

Simple examples:
- Auto-email after a lead signs up
- Auto-reminders for payment due
- Auto-assigning leads to sales reps
- Auto-task creation in ClickUp or Trello

Use **TeleCRM** for sales tracking, **New Zenler** for onboarding or training, and **Zapier** to connect your apps — even **Google Forms + Sheets** can save hours.

Automation saves time, reduces errors, and frees your people for real thinking.

"Businesses that automate even 30% of their repetitive tasks grow 23% faster on average."

— [Source: MSME Digital Adoption Index, 2023]

---

3. Track the Right Numbers

If you want to scale, you need to measure what matters.

That doesn't mean drowning in reports.

It means tracking a few high-impact metrics weekly:

- Lead-to-order conversion rate

- On-time delivery %

- Average ticket size

- Customer retention rate

- Task turnaround time

- Inventory vs demand variance

Keep it simple—track on a shared sheet, review every Friday, and make decisions based on data, not drama.

4. Build Flexibility into Your Resources

Scalable businesses can absorb sudden growth.

That means:

- Cross-training your team (so no task depends on one person)

• Building vendor backups (so you're not stuck if someone disappears)

• Having part-time or freelance help, you can tap when orders spike

• Negotiating flexible credit terms to handle short-term cash crunches

Think like a military commander — always planning three steps ahead.

5. Scale Yourself: Delegate to Multiply

Here's the part founders hate... but need the most.

You can't scale if everything still flows through you.

You must start building a team that makes decisions without you.

Not reckless ones — but guided, empowered ones.

Start by delegating outcome ownership, not just tasks.

Instead of: *"Call this client and send the file."*

Say: *"Ensure the client is fully updated and ready for launch. Use your judgment."*

Trust takes time. But without it, you'll always be the speed limit in your business.

Quick Checklist: Are You Scale-Ready?

✅ Do 70% of your core processes have SOPs?

✅ Is at least 30% of your work automated?

✅ Are your team members cross-trained for key tasks?

✅ Do you track 3–5 key metrics weekly?

✅ Have you delegated at least three high-impact outcomes?

If not, don't panic. But do start.

"Scalability is not about growing bigger. It's about growing smarter — with less chaos and more control."

In the next section, we tackle the human side of growth.

Because systems are great — but they're useless without the right people behind them.

Let's explore how to **build a team that doesn't just manage growth — but drives it.**

Your Growth Is Only as Good as Your People:

Build a Team That Scales with You

Let me say something upfront — and this might sting a little.

Your business will *never* outgrow the strength of your team.

You could have the best strategy, the perfect systems, and even investor interest brewing...

But if your team can't execute consistently, take ownership, or handle growth — you're stuck.

"A great team can fix a broken system. But even the best system will crumble under a weak team."

Scaling is not just about hiring more people. It's about building a team that grows *with* the business — not one that becomes dead weight when things get serious.

The Founder Trap: Doing Too Much for Too Long

Most MSME founders (especially in India) suffer from a strange kind of pride:

- "Nobody can do it like me."
- "I have to do everything."
- "If I don't follow up, work won't be done."

Sound familiar?

In the early stages, this works. You *have* to do everything.

But if you're still operating this way at ₹5–10 crore revenue — you're the bottleneck now.

And here's the scariest part:

Your best team members will leave—not because of low pay but because they don't see growth, trust, or space.

From Workers to Warriors: Shift in Mindset

If you want to scale, you don't just need employees.

You need **mini-CEOs**. People who think, own, and act.

That means creating an environment where your team:

- Feels trusted and valued
- Has clarity on goals and roles
- Is trained to handle complexity
- Gets feedback regularly
- Sees a path for growth

Not every hire will become a star. But your job is to **create the soil where good people can grow.**

The Right Hiring Approach for a Scaling MSME

Let's face it — most MSMEs don't have fancy HR departments.

That's okay. But you *must* be intentional about hiring.

Here's a simple 3-part hiring lens I recommend:

1. Skill Fit – Can they do the job right now?
Look for:
- Past experience in similar roles

- Hands-on comfort with tools/processes you use
- Portfolio or trial task instead of just resume chat

2. Culture Fit – Will they thrive in your work style?
Ask:

- How do they handle deadlines?
- Do they like autonomy or need hand-holding?
- Can they handle constructive feedback?

3. Scalability Fit – Can they grow with the business?
Look for:

- Curiosity and hunger to learn
- Ability to work across departments if needed
- Willingness to take initiative without always being told

"Businesses that hire for attitude and train for skill have 37% higher team retention rates."

— [Source: PeopleStrong MSME Talent Report, 2022]

Don't Hire for Today — Hire for Six Months from Now

Here's a mindset shift that changed everything for one of my clients:

Stop hiring reactively. Start hiring proactively.

Instead of saying:

- "We need a dispatch executive now."

Say:

- "Who do we need to manage dispatch at 3X volume?"

It costs more now — yes. But it saves you **months of pain** when growth hits.

Also, if you delay hiring until you're drowning, you'll hire in a panic. And that's when mistakes happen.

The First Layer of Leaders

Once you reach a certain scale, you need **middle managers—** even if it's just one or two people.

These are the ones who:

- Keep daily operations flowing
- Solve team issues before they reach you
- Train juniors and reduce founder dependence
- Take weekly reviews seriously

Start grooming them early. Give them mini-projects. Let them shadow you. Slowly hand over authority.

Yes, it'll feel uncomfortable at first.

But that's what freedom looks like.

Daily, Weekly, Monthly: A Rhythm That Builds Culture

You don't need big HR systems to build a strong team—just consistency.

Here's a simple rhythm you can follow:

- **Daily** – Morning standup (15 mins): "What are you working on? Any blockers?"

- **Weekly** – Task check-in + progress board (30–45 mins)
- **Monthly** – One-on-one feedback + learning goals (30 mins per person)

This rhythm builds accountability. Visibility. And trust.

Over time, your team becomes self-managing — not self-destructing.

What If Someone Doesn't Improve?

Let's not be naïve. Not every team member will evolve.

But before you fire — ask:

- Have I clearly defined expectations?
- Have I trained them adequately?
- Have I given them feedback and time to adapt?

If yes — and still no results — then yes, **letting them go**

is okay.

Holding on to low performers costs your A-players their energy and motivation.

Quick Reflection: Building Your Dream Team

- Who on your team could take on more — with some coaching?
- What process or task is still stuck with *only you*?
- Are you hiring for scale — or just filling today's gap?

- Do your team members know how *their work* connects to the company's vision?

Think about this deeply. Because...

"Your next stage of growth isn't in your product. It's in your people."

The next section discusses **handling the growth pressure** without letting quality drop, or customers suffer.

Because growth is great, but if you can't manage rising demand... it can all slip away just as fast.

Handle the Heat:

Managing Rising Demand Without Crashing

Growth is exciting — no doubt about that.

But here's the part most MSMEs aren't prepared for:

Growth brings pressure. Real pressure.

More leads. More orders. More calls. More follow-ups. More complaints. More expectations.

And if your systems, team, and mindset aren't ready for it?

What should feel like a celebration... starts to feel like suffocation.

"Most MSMEs don't break from failure. They break from uncontrolled success."

Let's change that.

This section is your toolkit for **handling increased demand** — without losing your grip on quality, customers, or peace of mind.

The Growth Whiplash: Why Demand Feels Overwhelming

Getting more orders would feel great.

But in reality, it often brings:

- **Delayed deliveries**
- **Stressed team members**

- **More mistakes and rework**
- **Customer escalations**
- **Cash flow gaps (yes, even with more sales!)**

Why?

Because your **systems were built for "normal."** Not for the "next level."

And the growth didn't come with a pause button. It just *landed*.

Step 1: Create a Buffer — Before You Need It

Don't wait for a breakdown to build bandwidth.

Build it proactively by:

- Hiring 1–2 roles *before* you feel desperate
- Cross-training team members (especially for delivery and support roles)
- Keeping backup vendors or freelancers ready
- Blocking 10–20% of team time for surge handling

Think of it like a dam. You need space to absorb the flood — *before* it hits.

Step 2: Tier Your Customers & Priorities

When demand surges, **you can't treat everyone equally**.

Yes, I said it. And no, it's not bad service — it's smart service.

Create 2–3 customer tiers:

- **Tier 1: High-value clients or long-term customers**

- **Tier 2: Medium-size or first-time buyers**
- **Tier 3: Bulk but low-margin orders or trial clients**

When your capacity is stretched:

- Prioritize Tier 1 for the fastest support and delivery
- Communicate proactively with Tier 2
- Set clear timelines with Tier 3 and overdeliver later

This way, your most valuable relationships are always protected — even during chaos.

"MSMEs that implement customer tiering during growth phases see 28% higher retention rates in their top accounts."

— [Source: India SME Customer Success Report, 2023]

Step 3: Systemize the Repetitive Stuff

Don't waste time doing what software can do better during high-demand seasons.

Automate these immediately:
- **Lead follow-up emails**
- **Invoice and payment reminders**
- **Internal task assignments**
- **Onboarding steps like welcome emails or form submissions**

Use tools like:
- **TeleCRM** – Lead and sales automation

- **Zapier** – App-to-app workflow triggers
- **New Zenler** – Customer onboarding, client education
- **Google Forms + Sheets** – Instant data capture and centralization

Let humans do human work. Let tech do the rest.

Step 4: Communicate Like a Pro (Even When Delays Happen)

Your customers will forgive delays... but they won't forgive silence.

Here's how to handle growing expectations without losing trust:

- **Set expectations early** — "This will take 5–7 working days."

- **Give updates proactively** — "We're on Step 3 of 5. Delivery will be on time."

- **Acknowledge delays honestly** — "There's a 24-hour delay due to demand surge. Here's what we're doing about it."

- **Add a goodwill gesture** — A small bonus, discount, or thank-you note goes a long way.

Keep the relationship first — always.

Step 5: Protect Your Core Team from Burnout

When demand grows, your team feels it first.

And if they burn out? Everything crashes.

Here's how to protect them:

- Give them a say in workload planning
- Rotate high-pressure tasks every 2–3 days
- Acknowledge wins — even small ones
- Offer comp-offs or bonuses during peak times

- Reduce unnecessary meetings

Also, check in — not just on work, but on **how they're doing.**

Because tired minds make mistakes. Motivated minds move mountains.

Quick Exercise: Your Demand Readiness Score

Answer honestly:

- If orders doubled tomorrow, would our delivery system survive?

- Who are our top 10 clients — and do we have a plan to protect them during chaos?

- What three tasks can we automate this week to reduce pressure?

- How is team morale during high-load weeks?

- Do we have surge plans or hope things don't go wrong?

If even one answer made you pause — good. That's your starting point.

As we wrap up this chapter, you've now built a strong foundation:

✔ You've identified your bottlenecks

✔ Streamlined your systems

✔ Built scalable processes

✔ Strengthened your team

✔ And now, I have learned to manage the heat of rising demand

You're no longer winging it. You're **engineering growth**.

The next chapter will focus on the **external battlefield — the competitive market.**

Because even the best internal engine needs **differentiation** to win out there.

Let's learn how to stand out so boldly... that your market can't ignore you.

Chapter 3: Stand Out or Stay Stuck

De-Commoditise Your Business and Attract Better Clients

Let's talk about something that silently kills the growth of most MSMEs.

It's not a lack of leads.

It's not competition.

It's not even pricing.

It's **blending in.**

Your product may be good. Your service may be honest. Your pricing may be fair.

But if you **look, sound, and feel like everyone else** in your category — the market will treat you like another option.

And when that happens, one thing becomes unavoidable...

You start competing on price.

Welcome to the dangerous world of **commoditisation**.

Where your customers can't tell you apart from the rest.

Where their only question is, "How much will you charge?"

Where they treat you like a vendor — not a partner.

And in this price-war trap, even great businesses struggle to survive, let alone grow.

But here's the good news: **it's a trap you can escape.**

This chapter will show you exactly how to do that — step by step.

The Problem: "I'm Better Than My Competition... But Nobody Notices"

You've put in the effort. You've improved your product. You deliver on time.

You care more. You work harder.

But when you speak to a prospect, you hear:

- "We will let you know after comparing the prices..."
- "We are looking for many other options..."
- "XYZ is doing the same thing..."

Sound familiar?

You feel invisible. Undervalued. Frustrated.

Because deep down, you *know* you're better — but the market doesn't see it.

That's what this chapter will fix.

The Agitation: Commoditisation Kills Profits, Passion, and Progress

When your business gets commoditised, three painful things happen:

1. Your margins shrink

You're forced to match prices. You give discounts. You play a losing game.

2. Your confidence drops

You start questioning your value. Your team loses motivation. You say yes to bad clients just to keep moving.

3. Your growth gets stuck

You can't scale a business that keeps lowering prices to survive. Investors won't touch it. Talented people won't join it. And your energy gets drained just to stay afloat.

So how do you escape?

By learning how to **stand out so clearly**, your customer stops comparing... and starts choosing.

Let's walk you through what's coming in this powerful chapter.

3.1 The Bland Trap – Why Most Businesses Get Ignored

This section breaks down the brutal truth: most MSMEs look and sound alike.

You'll discover:

- Why your marketing may be sabotaging your value
- How generic language kills your uniqueness
- Why even good businesses get treated like commodities

We'll show you how to identify "bland messaging" in your brand — and what it's costing you in lost revenue.

You'll walk away with the mindset shift required to stand out.

3.2 Your Value, Clearly Stated – Build a UVP That Makes You Unforgettable

This section is the foundation.

You'll learn how to craft a powerful, **Unique Value Proposition (UVP)** — a simple, clear, customer-centric statement that answers the golden question:

"Why should I choose you and not someone else?"

We'll give you frameworks, formulas, and real-world MSME examples to help you build your UVP — even if you think you have nothing special.

By the end of this section, your messaging will be sharper, stronger, and far more attractive to your ideal clients.

3.3 Be Seen, Be Remembered – Build a Brand That Stands Out

Now that your message is clear, it's time to make your business **look and feel unique**.

This section shows you how to align your **visual identity, tone, and touchpoints** — so that your brand actually reflects your value.

You'll learn how to:

- Choose the right visuals for your brand personality

- Create consistency across your website, packaging, and content

- Avoid the common branding mistakes most MSMEs make

Because the market won't remember you unless you give them something **distinct** to remember.

3.4 Earn Trust, Gain Influence – Build Authority in Your Industry

Standing out isn't just about style. It's also about **substance**.

This section teaches you how to become a **trusted voice** in your niche — even if you're small.

You'll discover how to:

- Create educational content that attracts attention

- Share proof, results, and case studies that build confidence

- Position yourself as a problem-solver, not just a seller

When people trust you, they stop doubting your price and trust your advice.

3.5 Say It Right – Messaging That Connects, Converts & Builds Loyalty

Finally, we'll show you how to communicate in a way that **moves people to** act.

You'll learn:

- How to talk about your business so your customers say, "That's exactly what I need!"
- How to write headlines, pitches, and follow-ups that convert
- How to align your message with your customer's mindset — at every stage of the buyer journey

This section turns your marketing from a cost... into a **conversion machine**.

Escape the Sea of Sameness:

Stand Out or Stay Stuck

Let's start with a harsh truth.

Most businesses look the same. Sound the same. Sell the same.

And when that happens, there's only one thing left to compete: **price.**

Sound familiar?

Your product is solid. Your service is sincere. You've put in years of hard work.

But the market... it just doesn't *see* you.

You feel like you're always explaining, always convincing, always dropping rates to close the deal. Meanwhile, another company — maybe not even better than you — is charging more, getting noticed, and growing faster.

"In a crowded market, being good isn't enough. You have to be different — and memorable."

This chapter is about how to break that trap.

Why Most MSMEs Become Invisible

It's not because they don't work hard.

It's because they blend in.

They say the same things everyone else says:

- "Best quality at lowest price"
- "Customer satisfaction is our motto."
- "Trusted by thousands since 1998"

But none of that makes your business **remarkable**.

Your customer has heard those lines a hundred times before. They tune it out — and go straight to comparing on price.

That's the death zone. And we're going to help you escape it.

In this chapter, we'll show you how to:

- Spot what truly makes your business **different** (even if you think you're in a boring industry)

- Craft a **Unique Value Proposition** that speaks to your dream customer

- Build a **brand identity** that sticks in the mind

- Create **authority and trust** in your niche

- And market yourself in a way that feels authentic — not desperate

Because once you learn to stand out — really stand out — you don't just grow faster.

You stop chasing customers.

They start chasing you.

The Bland Trap – Why Most Businesses Get Ignored

You've probably seen this before — maybe you've even done it yourself.

You visit a few business websites in your industry and start reading the headlines...

- "Committed to Quality"
- "Trusted Since 1995"
- "Your One-Stop Solution"
- "Customer Satisfaction Guaranteed"

And then you ask yourself, *"What exactly do they do? Why should I choose them over anyone else?"*

Chances are, you can't tell.

Because nothing about them *stands out.*

Now, here's the scary part—this is exactly what your **customer**s will experience when they look at **your** business... if you haven't built true differentiation.

"If you sound like everyone else, you become invisible."

How Commoditization Creeps In (Without You Noticing)

No one *starts* a business thinking, "Let me just be average and blend in."

But over time, as competition grows, markets mature, and trends shift, many MSMEs slowly drift into sameness.

It starts small:

- You copy what a competitor is doing (because it seems to be working)

- You remove the bold parts of your message (to play it safe)

- You start talking about *what* you do... not *why* you're different

- You try to please everyone — and end up resonating with no one

And just like that, **you've become a commodity.**

Customers compare you purely on price, delivery time, or discount offers, not value, experience, or expertise.

What Makes a Business a "Commodity"?

Let's simplify it.

You become a **commodity** when:

- The customer can't clearly see why you're different

- Your offerings are similar to everyone else's

- You compete mostly on price or speed

- Your brand feels generic or forgettable

- The customer sees your category, not your identity

This is deadly for MSMEs because you end up:

- Doing more work for less money

- Attracting low-loyalty clients

- Fighting in a race to the bottom

- Struggling to scale or attract investors

And worst of all? You lose your confidence. Because deep down, you know you're better than what the market sees.

"Commoditisation is not about the product. It's about perception."

The Real Reason Customers Ignore You (Even If You're Good)

Let's say your product is top-notch.

You deliver on time. Your team is responsive. Your price is fair.

Still, you're not getting noticed. Leads are cold, referrals are rare, and repeat orders are slow.

Why?

Because **being good is not enough**, people need a reason to *remember* you.

That's where your **positioning** comes in.

It's the mental shelf where your customer places your brand.

And if your shelf is labelled "just like the others," you're done.

But if your shelf says "the only one who does XYZ," your value skyrockets.

Quiz Time: Are You Commoditised?

Answer honestly — Yes or No:

1. Can a customer clearly explain your difference in one sentence?
2. Do you attract clients who value your expertise — not just your price?

3.   Does your website or brochure immediately showcase what makes you special?

4.   Are there at least two things you offer that your top competitors don't?

5.   Are you known for something specific in your market or industry?

If you said "No" to 2 or more — don't worry. That's exactly what this chapter will fix.

The First Step to De-Commoditizing: Awareness

Before you learn how to differentiate, you need to acknowledge the trap you're in.

Look at your current marketing:

- Are your messages clear and bold — or vague and safe?
- Are your offers specific — or generic bundles?
- Are your visuals and brand identity distinct — or copy-paste?
- Is your tone confident and human — or formal and forgettable?

Remember: you can't fix what you don't admit.

And chances are, you're only **one or two shifts away** from standing out — powerfully.

Key Lesson: Don't Be the Best — Be the Only

This isn't about inventing a new product.

It's about carving a **unique space** in your customer's mind.

Something like:

- "The most transparent logistics partner for fragile goods"
- "The only eco-friendly printing press with 3-day delivery"
- "The go-to marketing agency for homegrown food brands"
- "India's #1 solar installer for dairy farms"

See the difference?

You've defined not just *what* you do—you've defined *who you do it for* and *how you're different.*

That's when price stops being the conversation.

Build a UVP That Makes You Unforgettable:

Let's start with a simple truth.

If someone visits your website, reads your brochure, or hears your sales pitch — and **still has to ask, "So what do you do exactly?"** ...you've already lost them.

Or worse... they understand what you do but not **why they should choose you** over five others doing the same thing.

That's where a powerful **UVP** — *Unique Value Proposition* — becomes your best sales tool.

"A good UVP doesn't just explain your business. It makes people feel like your business is *meant* for them."

So, What *Is* a UVP?

It's not your tagline. It's not your elevator pitch. It's not a fancy slogan cooked up by an agency.

Your **Unique Value Proposition** is the crystal-clear statement that tells your customer:

1. **What** you do
2. **Who** you do it for
3. **How** you do it differently (and better)
4. **Why** it matters to them

It removes the guesswork.

It removes confusion.

Most importantly, it removes the temptation to compare you only on price.

Why Most MSME UVPs Fall Flat

Let's look at a few examples I've seen (or heard) in real client meetings:

- "We're a one-stop solution for all your packaging needs."
- "We provide high-quality, affordable interior design services."
- "We're committed to innovation, excellence, and customer satisfaction."

And my first reaction is always: *Cool. But so is everyone else.*

These are *not* UVPs. These are **generic noise**s.

They might sound "safe" and "professional"... but forgettable.

The test of a great UVP? **It should make your dream customer pause and say: "Wait, that's exactly what I need."**

The 4-Part UVP Formula

If you're wondering how to write yours, use this simple structure:

[We help] + [specific target audience] + [achieve this result] + [through our unique approach/offering]

Let's break it down with examples:

- *"We help eco-conscious cafes create customised, sustainable packaging through our zero-waste production process."*
- *"We help homegrown skincare brands launch faster by handling product design, compliance, and packaging — all under one roof."*
- *"We help regional textile manufacturers sell globally using our eCommerce-ready catalogues and international shipping network."*

Notice something?

- They're **specific**
- They highlight a **pain point or goal**
- They promise a **clear result**
- They suggest **how** it's done differently

That's what makes them stick.

"Companies with a clear, niche-focused UVP are 47% more likely to grow revenue year-on-year."

— [Source: MSME Positioning & Perception Study, 2023]

Don't Just Be Clear. Be *Customer-Centric*.

Here's a common mistake: making the UVP all about *you.*

- "We are experts in logistics and inventory control."
- "We've been leaders in this industry for 20 years."

Good to know. But your customer is thinking — *what's in it for me?*

Reframe it like this:

- "We help eCommerce sellers fulfil orders faster with live inventory updates and same-day dispatch."
- "We help high-growth food brands eliminate supply chain delays with predictive stock management."

Same expertise — reframed in a way that makes the **customer** the hero.

How to Discover What Makes You Unique

You might be thinking: *"But I don't have anything special. Everyone else does what I do."*

Not true.

Your uniqueness might be hiding in:

- **Your speed** (e.g., fastest turnaround time)
- **Your specialisation** (e.g., you only serve a certain niche)
- **Your process** (e.g., one-step onboarding, no manual errors)
- **Your story** (e.g., woman-led, rural-based, socially driven)
- **Your results** (e.g., 94% repeat clients)
- **Your experience** (e.g., 10,000+ units shipped across 14 states)
- **Your client experience** (e.g., WhatsApp tracking + real-time updates)

If you still can't find it, **ask your top five customers** why they chose you and why they stayed.

Their answers will surprise you. And guide you.

Before You Move On...

Let's recap.

Your UVP is your loudest, clearest answer to the question:

👉 *"Why should I choose you — and not someone else?"*

If your answer is vague, you'll fade.

You'll stand out if your answer is bold, clear, and specific.

And in a world drowning in options, clarity is your sharpest weapon.

In the next section, we'll bring this UVP to life — through **brand visuals, messaging, and identity** that don't just say you're different...

They **look**, **feel**, and **sound** different too.

Because now that we know what makes you special — it's time the world sees it.

Build a Brand That Stands Out:

You've done the deep work.

You've escaped the commodity trap.

You've crafted a clear, specific, customer-focused UVP.

But now comes the next critical step — one that MSMEs often overlook.

You have to look, sound, and feel different.

Because let's face it — people judge your business *before* they speak to you. Sometimes, in seconds.

Your website, brochure, packaging, showroom, social media, and even invoice layout are important. All of it says something about your brand.

The question is — *is it saying what you want it to say?*

"If your business feels forgettable, people won't even get to hear your UVP."

This chapter is about translating your differences into **a brand identity that speaks for you — 24/7.**

What Branding Really Means (And What Doesn't)

Branding is not just your logo. Or your colours. Or your tagline.

It's not about looking "modern" or "corporate" for the sake of it.

Branding is **how your business is remembered.** It's the vibe. The personality. The emotional connection. It answers these silent questions your customer is always asking:

- Can I trust these people?
- Are they for someone like me?
- Do they care about quality?
- Will they understand my needs?

You're invisible if your branding doesn't answer these — even subconsciously.

Step 1: Define Your Brand Personality

If your business was a person, how would it behave?

Think about it. Is your brand:

- Friendly or formal?
- Premium or budget-friendly?
- Traditional or modern?
- Bold or soft-spoken?
- Techy or artisanal?

You can't be all things to all people. Choose who you are.

Consistency in tone, look and feel makes your brand **stick**.

Use these three words to define your brand style:

"We are [adjective], [adjective], and [adjective]."

Example: *"We are approachable, efficient, and modern."*

This becomes your **filter** for design, copy, photos, and customer interactions.

Step 2: Make Visuals That Reflect Your Identity

Let's talk about how your business *looks*—visual branding is often the first (and sometimes the only) impression.

Here are the basics every MSME should focus on:

✓ Logo

Clean, modern, and scalable, this is not clipart from 2007. Hire a designer or use Canva Pro if needed.

✓ Colours

Choose 2–3 brand colours max. Use them everywhere—on the website, packaging, emails, and uniforms. Consistency builds recall.

✓ Fonts

Pick 1–2 fonts. Use them for headings and body text. Avoid mixing styles unless you know what you're doing.

✓ Images

If possible, use real photos. If using stock images, pick ones that match your brand tone. Avoid cheesy "office handshake" photos.

"Consistent branding increases revenue by up to 33% — simply because customers remember and trust you more."

— [Source: India MSME Brand Perception Study, 2023]

Step 3: Speak with a Voice That Connects

Your visuals get attention. But your **words** build trust.

This is where tone of voice comes in — how your business speaks in all its communication.

It shows up in:

- Your About Us page
- Your product descriptions
- Your email responses
- Your WhatsApp replies
- Even your invoices and thank-you notes

Decide how you want to sound:

- Casual and chatty?
- Polished and expert?
- Inspiring and visionary?

Once you choose — **stick to it everywhere.**

Step 4: Align Every Touchpoint

Your brand isn't just on your website.

It shows up everywhere a customer interacts with you.

And your brand starts to feel real when they all speak the same language.

Quick Exercise: Brand Reality Check

Take 5 minutes to answer:

- Does our visual identity reflect who we are?
- Would our ideal client feel "seen" when they land on our homepage?
- Is our tone of voice consistent across our platforms?
- What's one touchpoint that feels outdated or "off-brand"?

Write your answers. Discuss with your team. Then, pick *one* area to fix this week.

"If your brand doesn't feel different, your price will always need to be."

In the next section, we'll go deeper into **trust and authority**.

Because now that you've caught the market's eye — it's time to win its heart.

We'll show you how to become a **thought leader** in your space. One who gets *chosen*, not just seen.

Build Authority in Your Industry:

You've done a lot so far.

You've clarified what makes you unique.

You've shaped a brand that's visually and verbally distinct.

And now you're ready to rise above your competition.

But here's the truth: **being different isn't enough. You also need to be trusted.**

In the eyes of your ideal client, being *known* is good...

Being *understood* is better...

But being *trusted*? That's what creates momentum.

"People don't buy from the best. They buy from the one they trust the most."

This chapter is about how to turn your business from *"just another option"* into *"the obvious choice."*

And the secret lies in one powerful word: **authority.**

What Is Authority (And Why Should You Care)?

Authority is what makes people lean in when you speak.

It makes potential clients take your quote seriously — even if you charge more. It's what turns cold leads into warm conversations.

Authority comes from **consistency, credibility, and contribution**.

It's not about bragging. It's not about shouting.

It's not about showing off your awards.

It's about showing your expertise, helping before selling, and **building a track record of results** — publicly and generously.

The 5 Pillars of Authority for MSMEs

Let's make this practical. If you want to build trust and stand out in your industry, focus on these five:

✓ **1.** Educational Content

Don't just advertise. **Educate.**

Show your knowledge by sharing:

- Tips your clients can apply today
- Mistakes to avoid
- Behind the scenes of how you solve problems
- Step-by-step breakdowns of your process
- Customer success stories (with learnings)

Use formats like:

- Short LinkedIn or WhatsApp posts
- Email newsletters
- Short videos or Reels
- Mini case studies
- Free guides or checklists

When you teach without asking for anything in return, you earn *authority*.

"MSMEs that publish educational content twice a month generate 52% more qualified leads over 6 months."

— [Source: SME Digital Engagement Study, 2023]

✅ **2.** Proof of Results

Talk is cheap. But *results* build confidence.

Show, don't just tell.

- Share before-and-after stats
- Use screenshots of real client feedback
- Record video testimonials (even shot casually on the phone!)
- Publish mini-case studies with metrics

Example:

⬤ *"Before: 3-day dispatch delays. After: 24-hour turnaround using our new process."*

⬤ *"Client reduced cost per lead by 38% after using our targeted ad strategy."*

Numbers speak. Show them.

✓ **3.** Third-Party Validation

It's one thing to say you're great. It's another when **others say it for you**.

Try to collect:

- Client testimonials
- Google Reviews
- LinkedIn recommendations
- Mentions in local press, podcasts, or industry blogs
- Endorsements from influencers (even micro ones!)

Bonus tip: Frame good reviews, hang them in your office, or highlight them on your website. This will let visitors *see* your track record.

✓ **4.** Thought Leadership

Position yourself as someone who *leads thinking* in your niche.

Even if you're small, you can own a "space" in people's minds.

Examples:

- The first to talk about eco-packaging in your region
- The expert in digitising traditional retail
- The most responsive customer service in industrial supplies

Own a belief. Advocate for a better way. Share bold opinions respectfully.

That's how people remember you.

☑ **5.** Consistency

This is the secret that most give up on.

You don't build authority by one viral post.

You build it by **showing up over and over again.**

Make it part of your rhythm:

- Block 1 hour every Friday to create content or reply to comments
- Assign a team member to collect testimonials every month
- Create a folder for screenshots, reviews, and wins
- Build a "trust wall" on your website/social media

Repetition builds reputation.

Quick Reflection: Your Trust Scorecard

Grab your notebook and score yourself 1 to 5 on the following:

Trust Signal	Score (1–5)
Client testimonials or reviews	
Educational content posted recently.	
Case studies or before/after results.	
Thought leadership or opinion-sharing	
Website/social proof (logos, awards)	

If your total is below 15 — you're not showing enough of your greatness.

Start with just one pillar this week. Build slowly.

**"Authority is built when you stop chasing customers —
and start leading them."**

In the next section, we'll translate this trust into **messaging
that converts**.

Once people trust you, you need to know **how to say the right
thing to the right person at the right time**—without sounding
pushy or fake.

Let's make your message *stick*... and sell.

Say It Right:

Messaging That Connects, Converts & Builds Loyalty

You've clarified your UVP.

You've polished your brand visuals.

You've built trust and authority in your space.

Now comes the moment that makes or breaks everything...

What exactly do you say when you speak to your customers?

Because the world doesn't give you much time.

People scroll fast. They skim. They judge in seconds.

You don't get 10 paragraphs to make your case.

That's why your **messaging**—the way you talk about your product, service, and value—must be *instant* and effective.

"Clear messaging doesn't just sell. It builds trust. It reduces friction. And it makes the decision easy."

Why Most MSME Messaging Fails (Even If the Product Is Good)

You'd be shocked how often this happens.

A great MSME...

Good product...

Good service...

Still struggling with growth. Why?

Because their messaging is either:

- Too vague ("We deliver excellence." Okay, but *how*?)
- Too technical ("ISO-certified end-to-end modular compliance systems..." Zzz...)
- Too me-focused ("We, we, we..." while the customer is thinking "What about me?")
- Too cluttered (logos, banners, 17 bullet points on one flyer)

Here's the golden rule: **if you confuse them, you lose.**

Step 1: Make It All About *Them*

Your customer is not thinking about your features.

They're thinking about *their problem.*

So, shift from "what we do" to "what you get."

Examples:

✗ *We provide digital marketing solutions*

✓ *We help local businesses get more walk-ins using smart, local ads*

✗ *We sell high-efficiency air filters*

✓ *We help hotels keep their rooms fresher — and their guests happier*

This simple shift from **features to benefits** changes everything.

Step 2: Use the Language Your Customer Already Uses

One mistake MSMEs make is trying to sound too "impressive."

You start using big words—industry jargon. Fancy acronyms. But real people don't talk like that.

Speak in their language. Use their words. Repeat their pain points. Echo their desires.

Where do you find this language?

- Customer WhatsApp chats
- Google reviews
- FAQs your team keeps answering
- Sales call transcripts
- Comments on your ads or social media

When your customer reads your copy and says, *"That's exactly what I was thinking,"* — you win.

Step 3: The Message Triangle

All your messaging should hit on these three pillars:

💡 Problem

What pain or friction does the customer have?

"Tired of chasing vendors who miss deadlines?"

🔥 Promise

What is the outcome or transformation you provide?

"We guarantee 3-day delivery — or we pay the courier fee."

🎯 Proof

What backs up your promise?

"Used by 120+ small businesses across nine cities."

Craft your ads, landing pages, and brochures using this triangle.

Step 4: Keep It Simple, Repeat It Often

You don't need to say 10 things.

You need to say one thing **10 times** — consistently, across platforms.

Pick 1–2 core messages and repeat them:

- On your website
- In your WhatsApp replies
- On your product labels
- In your sales calls
- On your team's t-shirts (yes, really!)

Repetition builds memory. And memory builds trust.

"Customers don't remember the best brand. They remember the most clearly communicated one."

— [Source: Indian Buyer Psychology Study, 2022]

Bonus Tip: Messaging for Different Stages

Not all customers are at the same stage.

Here's how to tailor your message:

Stage	Example Message
? Curious	"Wondering if solar is right for your small business?"
Considering	"Here's a 3-minute video showing our ₹0-down installation plan."
✔ Ready to decide	"Get a free audit this week — and ₹5,000 off your first order."

Match your message to their mindset.

Quick Exercise: Rewrite Your Core Message

Grab a pen and answer these:

- What is your customer's **biggest frustration**?
- What **result** do they truly want?
- What **doubts** do they have about working with you?
- What **evidence** can you offer to remove that doubt?

Now draft one message using this template:

"We help [who] get [what result] — without [biggest frustration]."

Example:

"We help restaurants fill tables on weekdays — without wasting money on ads."

Stick that message on your homepage, brochure, and email footer.

Let it do the talking.

Final Thoughts Before We Close This Chapter

Messaging is not fluff. It's not "nice to have."

It's the difference between being scrolled past... and being *remembered.*

So take the time to:

☑ Speak your customer's language

☑ Show clear benefits, not just features

☑ Repeat, repeat, repeat

☑ Inject proof, heart, and simplicity into everything you say

In the next chapter, we move beyond marketing and into **customer loyalty.**

Because getting noticed is great. But **getting remembered — and referred to — is what creates real growth.**

Let's explore how to turn first-time buyers into lifetime brand advocates.

Chapter 4: Turn Buyers into Believers

Build Loyalty That Lasts

Let's start with a brutal reality that many MSME founders don't like to admit:

Most businesses are addicted to new customers.

They spend all their time, money, and energy chasing new leads, running ads, posting daily, making cold calls, offering discounts, and launching offers.

But they forget one simple truth:

"The easiest sale you'll ever make is to someone who's already bought from you."

Still, most MSMEs treat their customers like one-time transactions.

As soon as the sale is made, the relationship ends. No follow-up. No engagement. No feedback. No delight. No loyalty. And then they wonder...

Why is our growth so slow? Why don't we get repeat business? Why aren't customers referring us?

The answer lies in one word: **Retention.**

This chapter is about building a business where customers come back and bring their friends with them.

Where loyalty isn't accidental, it's *engineered.*

Where your brand becomes more than a service provider — it becomes a trusted part of your customer's life or business.

The Real Cost of Ignoring Customer Loyalty

Let's look at the numbers.

- It costs 5–7 times more to acquire a new customer than to retain an existing one.
- Repeat customers normally spend 33% more than new customers.
- Loyal customers are 4X more likely to refer you to others.
- Investors and IPO analysts *always* consider your customer retention metrics a sign of business health.

So, if you're only focused on **new** sales, you're leaving massive money on the table.

And you're building your business on sand, not stone.

This Chapter Will Help You Fix That.

We'll show you how to go beyond the sale... and create a loyal customer base that becomes your **engine for growth**.

Let's preview what's coming in the five game-changing sections ahead:

4.1 Why Customer Retention Matters – The Compounding Effect of Loyalty

Most MSMEs celebrate the first sale like it's the finish line.

But it's actually the starting point.

This section explains how repeat customers quietly drive profitability—with less effort, higher margins, and more referrals.

We'll expose the hidden costs of customer churn and show you how one small shift in retention can dramatically impact your bottom line.

You'll see how loyalty creates **compounding returns** — just like investments do.

4.2 Creating a Customer-Centric Culture – From Service to Experience

Loyalty doesn't come from discounts.

It comes from how your customer *feels* during and after the experience.

This section is about building a **customer-first mindset** in your team and systems.

We'll show you:

- How to turn basic service into memorable experiences
- How to train your team to care (even when you're not watching)
- How to build small rituals that make customers feel seen, heard, and valued

When customers feel special, they don't just stay — they **brag** about you.

4.3 Implementing Effective Loyalty Programs – Beyond Points and Punch Cards

Not all loyalty programs work.

Most are boring, forgettable, or complicated.

This section will explore how to design **smart, simple, and irresistible loyalty mechanisms**—even for traditional MSMEs.

We'll cover:

- What types of rewards work in Indian markets
- How to structure tiered benefits for different customer levels
- How to use referral incentives without sounding desperate

You'll leave with ready-to-use loyalty frameworks you can plug into your business this week.

4.4 Collecting and Acting on Customer Feedback – Listening is a Superpower

Your customers are always talking.

The question is — *are you listening?*

This section focuses on building a system for feedback — not just complaints.

We'll teach you how to:

- Ask the right questions at the right time
- Turn feedback into improvement — not just reports
- Use surveys, calls, and casual chats as a source of product innovation and service improvement
- Create "feedback loops" that keep your business growing

Customers who feel heard stay longer. And spend more.

4.5 Turning Satisfied Customers into Brand Advocates – Let Them Market for You

Happy customers are your *best marketing team*. And the cheapest.

But they won't refer you unless you give them a reason, a story, and a system.

In this final section, we'll show you:

- How to turn testimonials into trust-builders
- How to make it easy for customers to refer you

- How to use stories of impact to build your brand
- How to create a "circle of loyalty" that feeds itself

This is how MSMEs grow beyond their founder's hustle — through a tribe of believers.

What You'll Walk Away With

By the end of this chapter, you won't just have customers.

You'll have **fans**.

You'll have **referrers**.

You'll have **repeat buyers** who increase your revenue while decreasing your stress.

Most importantly — you'll have a **sticky brand** that's hard to leave... and easy to love.

Turn the page, and let's start with the *real reason* customer retention makes or breaks your growth.

Why Customer Retention Matters:

The Compounding Effect of Loyalty

You worked hard to get the sale.

You followed up. You pitched. You offered the right price.

Finally, the customer said yes. Order done. Deal closed.

Now what?

If you're like most MSMEs, your attention immediately shifts to the next sale.

The next lead. The next inquiry. The next campaign.

But doing that ignores the most powerful asset you've already earned—**the customer you just served.**

"A new customer gives you revenue. A repeat customer builds your business."

Welcome to the forgotten art — and science — of **customer retention**.

The Real Cost of Always Chasing New Clients

It's exciting to close new deals. It gives a dopamine hit. It feels like forward motion.

But here's what most business owners don't realise:

- It costs **5–7 times more** to acquire a new customer than to keep an existing one.

- A 5% increase in customer retention can boost profits by **25% to 95%.**
- Repeat customers are **9x more likely** to convert than first-timers.
- They are more forgiving.
- They are less price-sensitive.
- And they refer **better leads.**

Yet MSMEs keep spending more on Facebook ads, marketplaces, exhibitions, influencers — all chasing fresh leads...

While **ignoring the goldmine** sitting on their customer list.

Why Customers Don't Come Back?

Here's the myth most business owners believe:

"A happy customer will always return."

Not true.

A happy customer will only return if:

1. They **remember** you at the right time
2. They **feel connected** to your brand
3. They believe it's **easier to buy again from you** than try someone new

However, in most MSMEs, none of these happen. Why?

Because:

- There's no system for post-sale engagement
- There's no loyalty program
- There's no "next step" offered
- The business becomes silent after the sale

And that silence becomes a gap — which your competitor fills.

The Retention Flywheel: Compounding Growth Over Time

Think of your business like a wheel.

New customers give it a push.

Repeat customers keep it spinning — with less effort.

Here's how the **retention flywheel** works:

1. **First-time customer** buys →
2. You deliver great service + follow-up →
3. They return →
4. You delight them again →
5. They refer someone →
6. The referred customer buys →
7. Cycle repeats.

Each repeat client reduces your marketing burden.

Each referral reduces your cost of acquisition.

Each loyal customer becomes a micro-marketer.

And slowly, your business starts to grow **without chasing.**

"Retention is the interest you earn on a great customer experience."

But Isn't This Only for Big Brands?

Not at all. Whether you're a Kirana store, a regional manufacturer, a coaching institute, or a B2B exporter — **loyalty pays.**

What matters is not your size. What matters is your **mindset**.

You don't need a fancy CRM or AI-powered loyalty engine. You need:

- A system to track past customers
- A reason for them to return
- A method to follow up consistently
- And a culture that treats customers like relationships
— not revenue lines

Even a small MSME with 200 past customers can double revenue by reactivating and retaining 30% of them.

Quick Quiz: Are You Retention-Ready?

Answer honestly:

☑ Do you track how many customers return after their first purchase?

☑ Do you know your Customer Lifetime Value (LTV)?

☑ Do you have a post-sale follow-up system?

☑ Do your existing customers hear from you regularly?

☑ Do you ask for repeat business — or wait for them to remember?

If you answered "No" to 2 or more...

It's time to stop running harder. And start retaining smarter.

Creating a Customer-Centric Culture:

Let's be real — most businesses don't lose customers because their product is bad.

They lose them because the **experience feels average. Forgettable. Cold.**

And in today's world, *average service = broken trust.*

Because your customers are no longer just comparing you to others in your industry.

They're comparing you to Amazon, Zomato, Swiggy, Apple, and Netflix—brands that have set the bar for what *ease, speed, and care* should be.

"Loyalty is not built on what you deliver. It's built on how you make people feel when you deliver it."

This section is about transforming your business from just "serving" customers...

To **delighting** them. From doing the job...

to **create experiences, they remember — and return for.**

And this shift doesn't require millions. It requires **intent. Culture. And consistency.**

Why Great Service Is No Longer Enough

Let's say you deliver what you promised.

On time. With no mistakes.

Isn't that enough?

Unfortunately,... no.

Because that's just **a basic expectation** now.

Your competitors are doing the same. Your customers expect it. That's the *entry fee*.

What earns loyalty is when you go beyond the transaction.

- When your customer support sounds human — not robotic
- When you follow up even when there's no issue
- When you remember their preferences
- When you thank them without selling again

That's what separates "good" from "wow."

Step 1: Define Your Customer Experience Promise

Most MSMEs train staff on *tasks* — not on *experience*.

They'll say: "Install within 24 hours." But they won't say: "Make the customer feel relaxed, heard, and informed."

Here's a simple exercise:

Finish this sentence — "Every customer should feel _______ after dealing with us."

Examples:

- "Every customer should feel taken care of."
- "Every customer should feel they got more than they paid for."

• "Every customer should feel like they matter."

Build your service process around that **feeling**, not just the checklist.

Step 2: Empower Your Frontline Team

Your staff is not just delivering a service.

They're **delivering your brand.**

And yet, most founders treat frontline workers like low-skill doers — not brand ambassadors.

Change that.

- Train them on tone of voice, empathy, and small gestures
- Give them the authority to solve small issues without escalation
- Teach them to *own* the customer, not just complete the job

A small act — a smile, a tip, a proactive call — creates a big memory.

And memory creates loyalty.

Step 3: Build Rituals That Humanise the Brand

Customers remember *how* you made them feel — not the transaction details. So, create small rituals in your business that make people smile.

Examples:

- A thank-you call 3 days after delivery

- A "Happy One Year with Us" message for repeat clients
- A festive greeting with a small surprise during Diwali
- A personalised note inside a product box
- A free upgrade or bonus just because "you've been with us for 6 months."

These don't cost much. But they pay you back — in trust, goodwill, and referrals.

"People forget the price. They remember how you made them feel."

Step 4: Turn Complaints into Conversations

No matter how good your service is, problems will happen.

But here's the secret: **handling a complaint well builds more trust than getting everything right the first time.**

Here's how to do it:

- Respond fast. Even a quick "We're on it" helps.
- Apologise sincerely — don't deflect or get defensive.
- Solve it with speed.
- Follow up afterwards to make sure the customer is okay.

Then, ask: *"Is there anything else we could've done better?"*

A complaint, handled well, becomes a **relationship deepener**.

Step 5: Make It a Company-Wide Culture

A customer-first mindset is not a department.

It's a **culture.**

Every team — sales, delivery, accounts, even admin — must see their job as part of the customer experience.

Create a weekly rhythm around this:

- A 15-minute "Customer Wow" meeting to share wins or shoutouts
- A monthly review of common customer complaints — and how to fix them
- A team-wide reward for the best customer compliment of the month

This creates pride. Ownership. And a standard everyone wants to live up to.

Quick Exercise: Audit Your Customer Experience

Answer these:

✓ Do we have a documented post-sale process?

✓ Do we follow up with customers *without* selling again?

✓ Does every customer touchpoint feel personal, warm, and professional?

☑ Are our team members trained on customer experience — not just tasks?

☑ Do we track repeat buyers and actively try to improve that number?

If not — this is your moment to upgrade.

Final Thought Before We Move On

Customers don't stay loyal to the cheapest brand.

They stay loyal to the one that **cares** the most.

So, go beyond transactions.

Turn your service into a memory.

Turn your customer into an ambassador.

In the next section, we'll explore how to reward that loyalty — through **smart, simple loyalty programs** that increase retention and referrals.

You've made them happy.

Now, let's make them stay.

Implement Effective Loyalty Programs:

You've delivered great service.

You've created memorable customer experiences.

Now what?

How do you make sure that your customer **comes back again — and again — without chasing them?**

How do you make repeat purchases the *default*, not the exception?

And how do you reward your best customers in a way that makes them feel special — not like just another number?

The answer lies in designing a **smart loyalty system.**

Not a dusty old punch card.

Not a generic "5% off on your 5th visit."

But a **strategy** that drives behaviour deepens trust and grows your revenue.

"Loyalty is not just about rewards. It's about being remembered, preferred, and chosen — every time."

Let's build that.

Why Most Loyalty Programs Don't Work

Let's face it — most MSME loyalty efforts are either:

✖ Too complicated

✖ Too boring

✖ Too hidden

✖ Or... they simply don't exist

You give a discount here or a freebie there, but there's no system, rhythm, or structure.

So what happens?

- Customers forget the offer.
- Team members don't promote it.
- And you end up spending more on acquiring new customers... again

Here's the truth: **a well-designed loyalty program doesn't just bring people back — it increases their spending and reduces your marketing costs.**

Step 1: Decide What Behaviour You Want to Reward

Loyalty isn't just about frequency.

You can design your program to encourage specific actions:

- **Repeat purchases** (standard loyalty metric)
- **Referrals** (turn customers into marketers)
- **Bulk orders or higher value** (incentivise bigger baskets)
- **Feedback and reviews** (build social proof)

- **Engagement** (WhatsApp group activity, surveys, etc.)

Start by asking:

"What 2–3 customer behaviours would help us grow faster if they happened more often?"

Then, build your rewards around those.

Step 2: Keep It Simple, Visible, and Desirable

The golden rule of a loyalty program?

If the customer doesn't understand it in 10 seconds — it won't work.

Here's how to get it right:

- Use a name — not just "loyalty program" (e.g. "Green Circle," "VIP Club," "Insider Pass")
- Make the rewards visible — on your website, invoices, counter, WhatsApp replies
- Keep the maths simple — points, milestones, or tiers
- Offer emotional as well as financial rewards (priority support, sneak previews, recognition)

And please — don't make them download an app just to access rewards. Keep it friction-free.

Sample Structures That Work for MSMEs:

1. Tiered Loyalty Model:

- *Bronze*: 0–₹5,000 annual spend → occasional discounts

- *Silver*: ₹5,001–₹15,000 → priority service + birthday voucher
- *Gold*: ₹15,001+ → free gift every quarter + insider deals

2. Points System:

- 1 point per ₹100 spent
- 100 points = ₹100 reward
- Double points on special days

3. Referral Bonus:

- Refer a friend → Both get ₹250 off the next order
- Give them a unique referral code or link

4. Repeat Buy Bonus:

- Buy again within 30 days → get 10% off
- After five orders →, a surprise gift or upgrade

"The best loyalty programs don't feel like promotions. They feel like appreciation."

Step 3: Train Your Team to Promote It

Even the best-designed program will flop if your team isn't on board.

They must know:

- What the rewards are

- Who's eligible
- How to track and redeem them
- How to talk about it confidently and consistently

Run a 30-minute internal session. Give cheat sheets. Print posters. Share FAQs.

Make it easy for them to explain — and exciting for them to sell.

You can even gamify it for your team:

"Who gets the most loyalty signups this week?" — reward them too.

Step 4: Surprise and Delight — Don't Just Discount

You don't always need to give ₹₹ to win loyalty.

In fact, **small, unexpected gestures** often go further.

Ideas:

- A handwritten thank-you note on order #3
- A free product sample on their birthday
- A WhatsApp message on their first anniversary as a customer
- A behind-the-scenes photo or video just for them

These little touches make your customer feel **seen. Valued. Connected.** That's what loyalty is built on.

Quick Loyalty Checklist

✅ Do we have a system to track repeat customers?

✅ Do we know our average repeat purchase rate?

☑ Have we defined customer tiers or reward milestones?

☑ Is our program easy to explain in one sentence?

☑ Do our team and customers know about it?

If not — start simple. But start this week.

Listening is a Superpower:

Collecting and Acting on Customer Feedback

Let's make one thing clear:

If you're not listening to your customers, someone else is.

And in today's competitive landscape, the brand that listens — wins.

Because your customers are constantly giving you feedback:

- In the words they use
- In the questions, they ask
- In the complaints, they don't voice directly
- In the way they reorder (or don't)
- In their silence, reactions, tone, and tiny gestures

But if you don't have a system to catch and use that feedback, you're not improving — you're guessing.

"Customer feedback is not criticism. It's a free business consultant — sent directly by your market."

This section is about transforming how your MSME listens, learns, and grows through feedback — without getting defensive, overwhelmed, or stuck.

The Cost of Not Listening

When feedback systems don't exist, MSMEs suffer quietly.

Here's how:

- You repeat the same mistakes and wonder why clients leave
- You lose high-value customers without warning
- You create new products or services that no one asked for
- You solve internal issues instead of customer pain points
- You miss golden opportunities for growth — hidden in customer words

Most importantly, you lose **trust**.

And once trust is gone, loyalty soon follows.

Step 1: Build Feedback into the Flow

Stop waiting for complaints.

Instead, make feedback **a normal part of the customer journey.**

Here's how to do it:

- After purchase, → Send a thank-you + short rating link (Google Form / WhatsApp poll)
- After delivery → Call or message: "Were you satisfied? Anything we could've done better?"
- After service, → Ask: "How was the experience from 1 to 10?"
- After 30 days → "Still happy? Anything you wish was different?"

Keep it conversational. Keep it short. Keep it sincere.

When customers feel their voice matters, they speak honestly — and stay longer.

Step 2: Ask the Right Questions (Not Just Ratings)

Too many businesses ask: *"How was your experience?"*

The reply? *"Fine."* That gives you nothing.

Instead, ask **targeted, specific questions** that reveal real insights.

Examples:

- What's one thing we did well?
- What's one thing we could improve?
- Were you clear on how to use the product/service?
- Did we meet your expectations? Why or why not?
- Would you refer us to others? If not, what would stop you?

Don't just collect stars. Collect **stories. Emotions. Clarity.**

Step 3: Make Feedback Easy (And Mobile-Friendly)

Your customer is busy.

If you make them open an email, log in, or fill in 10 questions — forget it.

So simplify.

- WhatsApp polls
- Google Forms with three quick questions
- One-click rating links in your SMS/email
- QR codes on packaging

- Feedback buttons on your website or invoice

The easier it is, the more responses you'll get — and the more accurate they'll be.

"MSMEs that use structured feedback loops improve customer retention by 30% within 6 months."

— [Source: SME Service Experience Report, 2023]

Step 4: Track, Analyse & Act — Don't Just Collect

Feedback is useless if it's buried in spreadsheets or screenshots.

Here's what to do instead:

1. Create a simple **Feedback Tracker Sheet**

Date	Customer Name	Feedback	Positive	Negative	Action Taken	Owner	Status

2. Review it **weekly** in team meetings
3. Categorise issues: product, delivery, behaviour, clarity, etc.
4. Assign owners to fix recurring issues
5. Celebrate improvements (customer shoutouts, testimonials)

Feedback should **drive action**, not just documentation.

Step 5: Close the Loop (And Win Loyalty)

This is where 90% of businesses drop the ball.

They collect feedback... but never tell the customer what happened next.

So fix that.

- If you improved something, **tell them.**
- If you changed a policy, **share that.**
- If you added a new feature, **credit the person who asked for it.**

Example:

⬤ "Thanks to your input, we've added a size guide on every product page — appreciate your help!"

⬤ "You asked, we listened: COD is now available in your area."

Customers **who see** their feedback in action become emotionally invested in your business.

They go from clients... to co-creators.

Quick Self-Audit: Are You Really Listening?

Ask yourself:

☑ Do we actively collect feedback at different stages?

☑ Are we asking deep questions, not just ratings?

☑ Are we tracking, analysing, and discussing patterns?

☑ Are we taking visible action on what we hear?

☑ Are we closing the loop with customers?

If not — you're missing out on one of the most powerful growth engines.

Turning Customers into Brand Advocates:

You've delighted your customers.

You've delivered consistent service.

You've even collected honest feedback and improved.

But here's the next big leap:

What if your customers didn't just return — but started bringing others with them?

That's the true power of **brand advocacy**.

No ads.

No influencers.

No pushy sales campaigns.

But real people, saying real things, to other real people — about *you*.

"Marketing brings you leads. Advocacy brings you trust."

This chapter is about turning happy customers into your loudest supporters — and building a growth engine powered by **word of mouth.**

The Problem: We Focus on Selling, Not Spreading

Most MSMEs believe once a customer buys, the job is done.

But the truth is — **a happy customer is not a loyal customer... until they've told someone else about you.**

That's the moment they move from *satisfied* to *invested*.

But if you don't create a path for that to happen — most people never refer.

Why? Because:

- You never asked.
- You never made it easy.
- You never gave a reason.
- You never stayed in touch.

So they move on. Quietly. Even though they liked you.

Step 1: Identify Your Silent Fans

Not all customers will become advocates.

But many already are — quietly.

Here's how to spot them:

- Repeat buyers
- High average order value
- Customers who leave long, detailed feedback
- Customers who tag you online or share your posts
- Clients who say, "I told my cousin/friend/colleague about you."

These people already trust you.

Now, you need to invite them into your **advocacy system.**

Step 2: Ask for the Referral (Without Feeling Awkward)

Most founders don't ask for referrals because it feels needy or salesy. It's not.

In fact, *most* customers are happy to refer — if you ask the right way.

Here's how:

- "We're so glad you had a good experience! Do you know someone else who'd benefit from the same?"
- "Referrals mean the world to small businesses like ours. Would you be open to sharing this with a friend?"
- "We've just launched a referral bonus — thought you'd be a perfect fit!"

You're not begging.

You're inviting them to *spread value*.

"92% of people trust referrals from people they know. Only 33% trust ads."

— [Source: Nielsen Global Trust in Advertising Survey]

Step 3: Make Referring Easy and Rewarding

Here's the golden rule: **remove friction.**

Your customer shouldn't have to explain your business, write a custom message, or feel confused about what happens next.

Make it *super* simple:

- Create a ready-to-forward WhatsApp message or link
- Add a CTA at the bottom of your invoice or email
- Include a "Refer a Friend" card in every order
- Create a short, trackable referral code (e.g. RAVI100)
- Set up a form on your website with the name/email of the referee

And then reward them — *both of them.*

Examples:

- ₹100 credit for both (like PhonePe or Zomato)
- Gift or upgrade after three successful referrals
- Feature them on your Instagram as a "Top Referrer of the Month."

Recognition > Rupees. Rewards are good. But being appreciated? That's powerful.

Step 4: Turn Testimonials into Trust

Every time a customer says something good — don't just smile.

Capture it. Share it. Multiply it.

Here's how:

- Ask if you can quote them
- Take a screenshot of their WhatsApp message
- Record a 30-second testimonial video

- Post before/after photos (especially for physical products/services)
- Create "client story" posts showing their journey with you

Add these everywhere:

- Website
- Social media
- Proposals
- Brochures
- WhatsApp catalog
- Store walls

Let your future customers *see* how past customers feel.

Step 5: Create a Referral Culture Inside Your Team

Don't stop at your customers.

Your team can be powerful brand ambassadors, too — if you empower them.

- Give them referral links to share in their network
- Run a "Team Referral Challenge" with monthly rewards
- Encourage them to collect feedback and testimonials on the spot
- Celebrate employees when their referrals bring in new business

These builds pride. Momentum. Loyalty — *inside* your business, too.

Quick Self-Check: Are You Referral-Ready?

☑ Do we ask happy customers to refer others?

☑ Do we offer rewards or recognition for referrals?

☑ Do we have a system to track where referrals come from?

☑ Do we share our customer success stories publicly?

☑ Do our team members actively refer and promote the business?

If not — now's the time to build your referral engine.

Final Words Before We Close the Chapter

Your customers are not just your buyers.

They are your **marketers. Your storytellers. Your growth teams.**

If you treat them with care, make them feel special, and give them reasons to talk — they will.

And when they do, your growth becomes:

- Cheaper
- Faster
- Stickier
- Stronger

Turn satisfied clients into **believers**.

Turn believers into **advocates**.

And let your business become the one they **can't wait to recommend.**

Because that's not just loyalty.

That's *legacy*.

Chapter 5: Multiply Your Reach

Build a Smart, Sustainable Marketing Engine

You've strengthened your internal systems.
You've delighted customers and built loyalty.
You've turned happy buyers into your marketing team.

But there's one more crucial piece left.

Visibility.

Because no matter how good your product is...
No matter how great your customer experience is...
No matter how refined your operations are...

If new people aren't discovering your business consistently —
growth becomes stagnant.

"You can't grow a business that nobody knows about."

And yet, most MSMEs struggle with visibility.

They either:

- Spend too much money on ads with no ROI
- Waste time on social media without a strategy
- Rely solely on word-of-mouth and hope for the best
- Or do nothing, because "marketing is too confusing or expensive"

The result?
Low inquiries. Inconsistent sales. Stressful months.

But marketing doesn't have to be overwhelming, expensive, or risky.

In fact, with the right systems — marketing can become your **most powerful engine** for sustainable, scalable growth.

This chapter shows you how.

The Problem: Most MSMEs Market Without a System

Here's what marketing often looks like in a typical MSME:

- A few Instagram posts every now and then
- Some boosted Facebook ads during festive season
- Occasional pamphlets or hoardings
- Random messages sent on WhatsApp groups
- One-time email blasts with zero follow-up

No consistency. No clarity. No tracking. Just guesswork and hope. And hope, unfortunately, is **not a strategy.**

The Agitation: Lack of Visibility = Lack of Growth

Without a marketing system:

- You're stuck in survival mode
- Your team is under pressure to "somehow bring in leads"
- You have no control over demand generation
- You can't scale with confidence
- You depend on referrals, luck, and external forces

Worst of all, you miss out on customers who *want* what you offer — but don't even know you exist.

It's not a product problem. It's a **visibility gap**.

And we're going to fix it.

The Solution: Build a Smart Marketing Engine

This chapter will help you build a **sustainable marketing system** — one that:

- Attracts your ideal audience
- Positions you as the expert
- Builds trust before the first sale
- Brings in leads consistently
- And grows with you — without breaking the bank

Let's walk through what's coming in the five powerful sections ahead.

5.1 Start with Strategy – Don't Market Like Everyone Else

Most MSMEs jump straight into tactics: "Let's run Facebook ads!" or "Let's post reels!"

But smart marketing begins with clarity.

In this section, we'll help you:

- Define your ideal customer clearly
- Understand what truly motivates them to buy
- Craft messaging that attracts and qualifies the right people
- Set clear goals for visibility, leads, and conversions

You'll stop wasting time on activities that don't serve your business — and start building a strategy that compounds.

5.2 Create Magnetic Content – Attract, Don't Chase

You don't have to beg for attention. You just have to **earn it.**

This section is about how to create simple, effective, and low-cost content that pulls people in.

We'll show you:

- What kind of content works best for MSMEs
- How to use education, storytelling, and proof to build trust
- Where to publish — based on where your customers actually spend time
- How to batch, schedule, and repurpose content like a pro

You'll walk away with a weekly content rhythm that doesn't feel overwhelming — but works.

5.3 Use Organic Channels First – Build Trust Before Spending

Before you pour money into ads, make sure your free engines are working.

This section shows you how to leverage organic channels like:

- WhatsApp
- Google Business Profile
- LinkedIn or Instagram
- Email marketing
- Your own website or blog

We'll help you build a strong foundation of **free visibility** — so your brand grows even when your ad budget is ₹0.

Because trust built organically is trust that lasts.

5.4 Scale with Ads – But Without Wasting Money

When you're ready to scale, paid ads can be powerful — *if* you do it right.

This section breaks down:

- How to run simple, high-ROI ads on Meta and Google
- How to avoid common MSME ad mistakes
- How to test, track, and tweak your campaigns
- How to make sure your ads don't just bring clicks — but **clients**

Whether your budget is ₹1,000/month or ₹1 lakh/month, you'll learn how to make every rupee count.

5.5 Measure What Matters – Track, Improve, Repeat

What gets measured, gets improved. In this final section, we'll show you how to:

- Set up a simple marketing dashboard
- Track key metrics (reach, leads, conversion, CAC, ROI)
- Spot what's working — and double down
- Stop what's draining money and energy
- Build a review rhythm that keeps your marketing sharp

Because marketing isn't a one-time event. It's a **living system** — and systems need monitoring.

What You'll Gain from This Chapter

By the end of Chapter 5, you'll have:

- ✅ A crystal-clear marketing strategy
- ✅ A weekly content plan that builds trust
- ✅ Strong organic visibility without burnout
- ✅ Paid campaigns that actually convert
- ✅ A dashboard to track, optimise, and grow

Most importantly — you'll have **control.**

Control over your visibility. Control over your leads. Control over your business growth. Let's build a marketing engine that works **for you** — not the other way around.

Don't Market Like Everyone Else:

Marketing is not a to-do item. It's not something you "start doing" once business slows down.

It's not an Instagram post here, a WhatsApp blast there, and a few boosted ads during Diwali.

Marketing is the engine.

And like any engine, it needs a proper **design** — not random wires and fuel thrown together.

"If you market without strategy, you'll either waste money or attract the wrong people — or both."

That's where most MSMEs go wrong.

They look at what their competitors are doing.
They copy without context.
And when it doesn't work, they say, "Marketing doesn't work for us."

Wrong.

It's not that marketing doesn't work — it's that **strategy was missing**.

This section will help you lay the foundation of a **smart, customised, result-driven marketing strategy** that brings the right people, builds trust, and supports your long-term goals.

Let's begin.

The Problem: Tactics Without a Target

Here's how most MSMEs approach marketing:

- "Let's run Facebook ads for ₹5,000."
- "We need more followers on Instagram."
- "Print some new flyers — business is slow."
- "We should post videos, everyone's doing that."

Notice a pattern?

All tactics. No target.

Marketing becomes an activity — not a system.

There's no clarity on:

- Who the message is for
- What problem it solves
- What result is expected
- How to measure success
- What makes it different from competitors

It's like trying to shoot arrows in the dark — you might hit something by accident, but it's not repeatable.

Step 1: Identify Your Dream Customer Clearly

Let's be honest.

You don't need *more* leads. You need the *right* leads.

And for that, you need to know exactly who you're talking to.

Ask:

- Who benefits most from your product or service?
- Who has the budget and urgency to buy?
- Who is already buying from your competitors?
- What's their daily struggle that your business solves?

Build a **Customer Profile Card**:

Attribute	Description
Age/Role	Factory owner, 35–50 yrs
Location	Industrial belts in Maharashtra
Pain Point	High energy costs, unreliable service
Aspiration	Save money, run a greener business
Where They Hang Out	LinkedIn, Trade WhatsApp groups

This is your "Dream Buyer." Every campaign, every message should be built for *them*.

Step 2: Clarify Your Core Promise

Your message should answer one simple question:

"Why should I buy from you, and not from someone else?"

Not in paragraphs. In one sentence.

Examples:

> - *"We help retail shops boost footfall with zero-waste, location-based advertising."*
> - *"We deliver custom printed packaging in 72 hours — or we pay the courier charges."*
> - *"We help boutique cafes automate their social media — no agency required."*

This is not a slogan. This is your **Core Marketing Statement.**

Put it on your homepage. Your pitch. Your flyers. Your ads. It becomes your marketing spine.

Step 3: Define Your Success Metrics

If you can't measure it, you can't improve it.

What does successful marketing look like for *you*?

Choose 2–3 key metrics to track:

Goal	Metric
Awareness	Reach, impressions, profile visits
Engagement	Comments, replies, shares
Lead Generation	New inquiries, form fills, DMs
Conversion	Sales from leads
Cost Efficiency	Cost per lead / customer

Track these weekly. Discuss them monthly. Improve them quarterly.

Without metrics, marketing becomes emotional — "I think it's working."
With metrics, it becomes logical — "We improved leads by 22% last month."

Step 4: Choose the Right Platforms — Based on Your Audience

You don't need to be everywhere.

You need to be where your dream customers are — consistently, with clarity.

Choose your core 2–3 channels based on your audience's habits:

- **WhatsApp** – For re-engagement, follow-ups, and customer nurturing
- **Google Business Profile** – For local discovery and trust
- **LinkedIn** – For B2B and professional services
- **Instagram** – For visual brands, lifestyle, and youth markets
- **YouTube** – For education-based marketing
- **Email** – For nurturing long-term, high-value leads

One channel done well beats five done poorly.

"Clarity beats complexity. The best marketing strategies are simple, sharp, and repeatable."

Step 5: Align Marketing with Business Goals

Your marketing is not a side hustle. It must serve your **core business priorities.**

Ask yourself:

- Are we launching a new product soon?
- Do we want to target a new customer segment?
- Are we trying to build authority in our space?
- Do we need short-term cash flow or long-term brand growth?

Once you know the business goal — the marketing strategy becomes clear.

Marketing must follow business priorities — not the latest trend.

Quick Recap & Action Plan

- ☑ Define your Dream Customer
- ☑ Craft your Core Marketing Statement
- ☑ Select 2–3 Key Metrics
- ☑ Choose your 2 Primary Channels
- ☑ Align campaigns with business goals

You don't need to be everywhere. You need to be *intentional*.

Create Magnetic Content:

Attract, Don't Chase

Imagine this.

Your ideal customer is scrolling their phone.
They're tired of ads. Suspicious of salespeople. Ignoring cold DMs.

And then, they see something that stops them.

A short post that speaks their exact problem.
A video that explains their struggle better than they could.
A reel that makes them nod in agreement.
A client story that makes them think, *"This is the brand for me."*

That's not magic. That's **magnetic content**.

"Good content doesn't just inform — it attracts, connects, and converts."

In this section, we'll show you how to create the kind of content that doesn't just fill your feed — but fills your pipeline.

The Problem: Most MSMEs Create Content That Gets Ignored

Let's be blunt.

Most content by MSMEs looks like this:

- "New product launch! DM now."
- "Best quality at best price."
- "10% off till Sunday. Hurry!"
- "Follow us for more updates!"

It's pushy. It's repetitive. It sounds like every other business.

The result?

- Low engagement
- No shares
- No trust
- No leads

Because people don't log in to social media to be sold to. They log in to be **entertained, informed, inspired, or educated**.

If your content doesn't serve one of those purposes — it's invisible.

The Agitation: Without Content, You're Always Chasing

Think about it.

If your brand has no presence...
If your expertise isn't visible...
If your story isn't shared...
If your customers aren't talking about you...

Then who *is*?

Without good content:

- You have to chase leads manually
- You rely only on ads (expensive) or cold calls (time-consuming)
- You get compared only on price
- You have no brand equity

You become replaceable.

And that's what magnetic content helps you avoid.

Step 1: Understand What Content Actually Does

Content is not about showing off.

It's about **building trust at scale**.

Here's what great content does:

- Attracts your ideal customer
- Educates them on their problem
- Positions you as the expert
- Pre-sells your product or service
- Keeps you top-of-mind when they're ready to buy

It's your **silent salesperson** — working 24/7.

Step 2: Choose Your Core Content Types

You don't have to be on every platform or create every format.

Pick 2–3 types based on your audience and comfort.

One idea → Five assets → Multiple platforms.

Here's a simple menu:

Format	What It Does	Best For
Carousel Posts	Teach step-by-step concepts	Instagram, LinkedIn
Short Reels	Entertain or show behind-the-scenes	Instagram, YouTube Shorts
Explainer Videos	Educate about process or problems	YouTube, LinkedIn
Stories	Build personal connection, show process	WhatsApp, Instagram
Blog Posts	Build SEO + long-form authority	Website, Email
Testimonials	Build trust through proof	All platforms

Start with one long-form (like a blog or video) and repurpose it into multiple short-form pieces.

One idea → Five assets → Multiple platforms.

Step 3: Use the 4E Content Framework

Every great piece of content does at least one of these:

☑ Educate

Teach your audience something useful.
E.g. "3 things to check before hiring a marketing agency"

☑ Entertain

Make them smile, laugh, or nod.
E.g. A reel showing common customer mistakes in a fun way

☑ Empathize

Show them you understand their problem deeply.
E.g. "You've tried five vendors. Still no results? You're not alone."

☑ Establish Trust

Show proof, results, testimonials.
E.g. "How we helped this retail brand grow footfall by 27% in 45 days"

Plan your weekly content calendar around these 4Es.

Step 4: Keep the Language Simple, Relatable, and Real

Please don't write like a corporate brochure.

Instead, write like a human.

- Use real words. Not jargon.
- Use "you" more than "we"

- Use visuals — photos, infographics, demos
- Speak like you'd speak to a customer sitting across the table

The more real you sound, the more relatable you become.

And people buy from brands they relate to.

"People don't want more information. They want clarity and connection."

Step 5: Show Up Consistently, Not Perfectly

You don't need viral content.

You need **valuable, consistent content**.

- Post 2–3 times a week
- Reuse old content in new formats
- Reply to comments and DMs
- Show your face, your team, your process

Start small. Show up often. Stay human.

Trust builds over time — not in one post.

Quick Content Ideas You Can Use This Week

☑ "Behind the scenes of how we package your orders"
☑ "3 signs your vendor is overcharging you"

☑ "Before/after of a client project"

☑ "Customer review + founder reaction"

☑ "A quick lesson we learned this week in business"

These work because they're **real. Specific. Story-driven.**

Build Trust Before Spending:

Imagine you walk into a store and the salesman immediately says:
"Sir, 20% off — take it today!"

No conversation. No understanding. Just pressure.

You'd likely feel irritated or walk away, right?

That's exactly how your customers feel when MSMEs rush into paid ads **without first building trust.**

"Before you ask for attention through ads, earn it through value."

Organic marketing is how you do that.
It's the quiet but powerful way to attract, engage, and build long-term relationships — *before* you spend even one rupee.

This chapter will help you create a strong foundation using **free, trust-building channels** that work for Indian MSMEs.

Because smart businesses don't just grow wide. They grow deep.

The Problem: Paid Ads Without a Warm Audience = Waste

Most MSMEs follow this pattern:

1. Business is slow
2. Panic sets in

3. Someone suggests, "Let's run Facebook ads"
4. ₹5,000 spent
5. 200 clicks, 10 inquiries, 0 conversions
6. Conclusion: "Digital marketing doesn't work for us"

The truth?

The **audience wasn't ready.**

No brand awareness.
No trust.
No familiarity.
No warmth.

Paid traffic to a cold audience is like proposing marriage on the first date.

Organic channels warm people up — so when they finally see your ad, they're already half-convinced.

Step 1: WhatsApp – Your Most Powerful Organic Tool

For Indian MSMEs, **WhatsApp is not a chat app. It's a business engine.**

Here's how to use it right:

✅ Broadcast Lists (Not Groups)

Send regular updates, tips, offers, and behind-the-scenes content to your list.

Keep it:

- Short
- Friendly
- Value-driven
- 1–2 messages a week

✓ WhatsApp Catalogue

Upload your products or services. Add prices, photos, short descriptions. Send direct links in replies.

✓ Status Updates

Use your Status to show:

- Customer testimonials
- Work-in-progress clips
- Founder thoughts
- Flash offers
- Process insights

People who view your status regularly = warm leads.

✓ Use a WhatsApp CRM

Tools like TeleCRM or WA Sender can help manage follow-ups, reminders, and conversations at scale.

Step 2: Google Business Profile – Win Local Search

If your business depends on **local visibility** — Google is your gateway.

Most people today search:
"Best bakery near me"
"Wedding photographer in Surat"
"Electrician open now"

If you're not showing up, your competitor is.

How to Optimise:

- Add real photos (team, premises, product, clients)
- Write a keyword-rich description
- Update business hours
- Add WhatsApp/call button
- Post weekly updates — offers, projects, new arrivals
- Actively request Google reviews after every transaction

More reviews = more trust = more calls.

Step 3: LinkedIn or Instagram – Choose Based on Audience

You don't need both. Choose based on your market.

If you're B2B or serve professionals: Go LinkedIn

Post 2–3 times a week:

- Industry insights
- Client results
- Educational carousels
- Founder journey stories
- Collaboration shout-outs

Engage with comments. DM warm leads. Build authority.

If you're B2C, creative, or lifestyle-based: Go Instagram

Focus on:

- Reels (behind-the-scenes, quick tips, relatable humour)
- Carousels (before/after, how-to, storytelling)
- Stories (daily updates, polls, replies, customer moments)

Instagram builds **familiarity**. And familiarity leads to **follow-through**.

Step 4: Email Marketing – The Most Ignored Superpower

Email feels old-school. But it works. While social platforms can shut down your reach, your email list is **yours**.

Start by:

- Collecting emails from every buyer, lead, and website visitor
- Using free tools like Mailchimp or ConvertKit
- Sending weekly/bi-weekly newsletters with:
  - Useful tips
  - Product updates
  - Offers
  - Customer stories
  - Founder messages

Emails build *relationship equity*. Quietly. Consistently.

Step 5: Your Website – Not a Brochure, But a Conversion Tool

Too many MSME websites are digital business cards — not marketing machines.

Here's how to fix that:

- Clear headline with your UVP (Unique Value Proposition)
- Social proof: reviews, testimonials, client logos
- Lead magnet: free guide, consultation, or trial
- WhatsApp button or inquiry form
- Real photos and stories — not stock images
- Mobile-first design

Treat your website as your **best salesperson** — always ready.

Quick Action Checklist: Your Organic Engine

- ✅ WhatsApp Broadcast + Status rhythm
- ✅ Google Profile fully updated with reviews
- ✅ One social media channel done consistently
- ✅ Weekly email to your subscriber list
- ✅ Website optimised for trust + lead generation

If even 3 out of 5 are running smoothly — you'll start seeing results before touching paid ads.

Scale with Ads:

Let's begin with a harsh truth:

Most MSMEs burn money on ads.

Not because ads are bad.
But because there's **no strategy**, no system, and no patience.

They boost a post randomly.
They run a campaign without tracking.
They hire an agency without clarity.
They target "everyone" — and reach no one.

Then they say: *"Facebook loot raha hai. Google kuch return nahi de raha."*

The problem isn't the platform.
The problem is the **approach**.

"Paid ads don't fix a broken funnel — they just expose it faster."

This chapter will help you scale smartly with ads.
No guesswork. No jargon. No blind spending.
Just clear, controlled campaigns that turn rupees into results.

The Problem: Most MSMEs Spend Before They're Ready

Imagine this:

You just set up a new shop.
No signage. No lighting. No trained staff.
Would you print 10,000 flyers and invite the city?

Of course not.

But that's what MSMEs do when they run ads **before fixing their messaging, offer, and follow-up.**

Here's what typically happens:

- Ad brings in a few clicks
- Landing page is slow or unclear
- Lead fills a form, gets no response
- Team forgets to follow up
- Business owner loses money and hope

It's not an ad problem. It's a **system problem.**

Ads amplify what already exists — good or bad.

The Agitation: Poor Ads Create Poor Impressions

When your ad:

- Looks like spam
- Targets the wrong people
- Sends traffic to a dead-end
- Fails to connect emotionally
- Or gets no follow-up...

You don't just lose money. You lose **credibility.**

And in a world where attention is limited, every bad impression lower trust — even for future campaigns.

Step 1: Get the Foundation Right Before You Scale

Before running ads, ask yourself:

- ☑ Is your UVP clear and compelling?
- ☑ Is your content warm, consistent, and trust-building?
- ☑ Is your website/mobile page fast and mobile-friendly?
- ☑ Do you have a follow-up system (WhatsApp, CRM, calls)?
- ☑ Do you know your best-selling product/service?

If even two of these are shaky — pause. Fix them first. Only then does ad spend become **multiplication**, not **money loss.**

Step 2: Choose the Right Platform Based on Your Goal

Not all platforms serve the same purpose.

Platform	Best For	Campaign Type
Facebook/Instagram	B2C, local, lifestyle, impulse	Reach, Traffic, Engagement, Leads
Google Search	High-intent keywords	Search Ads, Local Campaigns
Google Display	Brand awareness	Banner Ads, Retargeting
YouTube	Educational, visual explainer	Skippable Ads, Shorts
LinkedIn	B2B, high-ticket, niche	Lead Generation, Retargeting

Choose based on where your **audience** is — and what action you want them to take.

Step 3: Start with a Small, Testable Budget

Don't throw ₹50,000 into one campaign.
Start small. Test. Learn. Scale.

Suggested ad budget roadmap:

- **Month 1–2:** ₹5,000–₹10,000 → Test 2–3 creatives + audiences
- **Month 3–4:** ₹10,000–₹20,000 → Optimise based on conversions
- **Month 5+:** Scale what's working (₹30K+ based on ROI)

Track your **Cost per Lead (CPL)**, **Cost per Acquisition (CPA)**, and **Return on Ad Spend (ROAS)**.

What matters is not how much you spend? What matters is **what you get per ₹1 spent.**

Step 4: Craft Ads That Speak Like Humans, Not Banners

People don't click ads that scream "SALE!"

They click ads that:

- Call out their pain
- Promise a real benefit
- Feel personal, not promotional
- Show results, not fluff

Here's a simple copy formula:

[Call out the pain] → **[Show the promise]** → **[Add proof or urgency]** → **[Clear CTA]**

Example for a B2B IT firm:

Tired of IT issues eating into your team's productivity?
We help MSMEs run faster with managed IT support that works.
Trusted by 150+ small businesses.
Book a free 15-min audit today.

That's not advertising. That's **clarity.**

Step 5: Follow Up Like a Pro — Fast and Friendly

Your ad is just the beginning.

The sale happens in the **follow-up**.

- Use CRM tools like TeleCRM or LeadSquared
- Send a WhatsApp message within 5 minutes
- Call within 1 hour — don't wait for "later"
- Ask a question to continue the conversation
- Build rapport — don't just send a price list

Speed = Trust.
Personalisation = Connection.
Follow-up = Conversion.

Bonus: Retargeting — The Smartest Ad You'll Ever Run

Not everyone buys on the first click.
But they *might* after the second.

Run **retargeting ads** to people who:

- Visited your website
- Watched 50% of your video
- Engaged with your Instagram
- Added to cart but didn't buy

These ads cost less — and convert better.

Because they reach **warm leads** who already know you.

Quick Ads Health Checklist

- ☑ Clear campaign goal (reach, leads, traffic, sales)
- ☑ Platform chosen based on audience
- ☑ 2–3 ad creatives with emotional clarity
- ☑ Landing page or WhatsApp funnel working
- ☑ Follow-up system ready to respond fast
- ☑ Budget tracked weekly with CPL/ROAS insights

If all green? You're ready to scale.

Measure What Matters:

You've built a strategy.
You've created content.
You've activated organic channels.
You've even dipped your toes into paid ads.

But here's the million-rupee question:

What's working? And what's not?

If you can't answer that — you're not marketing. You're just experimenting blindly.

"If you don't measure, you can't improve. If you don't track, you can't scale."

And yet, most MSMEs are flying blind.

They post content without checking performance.
They run ads without calculating returns.
They get inquiries but never measure conversion.
They think marketing is "working" because the owner *feels* busy.

Feelings don't grow a business. **Data does.**

In this section, we'll help you set up a **simple, clear, MSME-friendly marketing dashboard** — so you can make smart decisions and grow without stress.

The Problem: MSMEs Rely on Gut-Feel, Not Metrics

Let's break down how typical MSMEs track marketing:

- "We got more calls this month. Must be working."
- "Our Instagram likes are down. Something's wrong."
- "Bhaiya, how many people saw our Google ad?"
- "Sales are slow. Maybe let's post more."

It's reactive. Vague. Based on mood or noise.

Without tracking:

- You don't know your best-performing channel
- You can't repeat what worked
- You keep guessing what to change
- You waste time, money, and energy

And worst of all — **you lose control.**

The Agitation: Lack of Metrics = Lack of Momentum

When you don't measure:

- You hesitate to spend more — because you don't trust the outcome

- Your team doesn't know what success looks like

- Your campaigns stay random — instead of being improved

- Your growth becomes inconsistent

You feel busy … But you are stuck.
You are visible. But not profitable.

Tracking doesn't slow you down.
It **frees you up** to do more of what actually works.

Step 1: Know the 6 Marketing Metrics That Matter

You don't need a 25-column spreadsheet.
You just need to track the *right* few numbers.

Here's your MSME Marketing Metric Set:

Metric	What It Tells You	How to Track
Reach	How many people saw your brand	Facebook/Instagram/Google insights
Leads	How many people showed real interest	CRM, WhatsApp logs, website forms
Cost Per Lead (CPL)	How much each lead cost you	Total ad spend ÷ number of leads
Conversion Rate	What % of leads became customers	Total sales ÷ total leads
Customer Acquisition Cost (CAC)	Full cost to get one buyer	Ad cost + time + salaries ÷ new buyers
Return on Ad Spend (ROAS)	Revenue earned per ₹1 spent on ads	Revenue from ad campaign ÷ ad spend

Tracking just these 6 gives you control over: Visibility, Efficiency, Sales performance, Profitability

Step 2: Build a Simple Monthly Dashboard

Here's a basic structure you can use in Excel, Google Sheets, or tools like Notion or Airtable:

Month	Reach	Leads	CPL	Sales	CAC	ROAS
Jan	10,000	120	₹42	35	₹145	3.2x
Feb	15,000	180	₹38	47	₹132	3.8x
Mar	9,000	80	₹56	21	₹178	2.1x

Colour-code it. Track trends. Spot red flags.

Review it on the **1st of every month** with your team.

Ask:

- Which channel gave us the most leads?
- Which campaign gave us the lowest CPL?
- Are our conversion rates improving?
- Is our CAC getting cheaper or costlier?

These discussions lead to decisions.
And **decisions create growth.**

Step 3: Track Per Channel to Know What to Double Down

Don't just track total numbers.
Track per platform — so you know where to focus.

Channel	Leads	CPL	Conversion	ROAS
WhatsApp	45	₹20	25%	4.2x
Instagram	88	₹38	12%	2.5x
Google Ads	34	₹52	20%	3.1x

This tells you:

- Where your **cheapest leads** come from
- Where your **best converting leads** come from
- Where to **cut waste** and where to **scale**

Even small MSMEs can do this once a week in a 15-minute review.

No fancy tools. Just intention and habit.

Step 4: Set Monthly Goals and Compare

What gets tracked can be **benchmarked**.

Set monthly goals like:

- "This month, let's get 100 leads at under ₹40 CPL."
- "We'll aim for ₹1.5 lakh revenue from ₹30K ad spend (5x ROAS)."

- "Let's improve conversion rate from 12% to 15%."

Review them. Adjust campaigns. Tweak messaging. Make marketing **a scoreboard**, not a mystery.

Step 5: Keep It Founder-Friendly

This is key.

You don't need to become a data scientist.

Just make sure your dashboard is:

- Easy to update weekly
- Clear at a glance
- Shared with your team
- Focused only on *growth-driving numbers*
- Not overloaded with vanity metrics (likes, followers, etc.)

Your goal is **actionable clarity**, not complexity.

Final Thought: What You Measure, You Multiply

If you want growth on demand — not by chance — you need visibility into your numbers.

- ✅ Leads
- ✅ Costs
- ✅ Returns
- ✅ Conversions

This is how you stop wasting money.
This is how you grow confidently.
This is how you **scale sustainably.**

Wrap-Up: What You've Built in This Chapter

You now have:

- A clear marketing strategy
- Magnetic content
- An organic engine
- Profitable ads
- And a tracking system that powers smart decisions

This is not just marketing. This is **momentum.**

Keep it consistent. Review monthly. Improve quarterly.

In the next chapter, we'll shift from visibility to **team systems** — because to scale further, your marketing needs support from **execution that doesn't rely on you alone.**

You've built a growth engine.
Now let's build the team that runs it.

Chapter 6: Build Systems, Not Stress

Every entrepreneur dreams of a business that grows without breaking. A business that doesn't need their presence in every decision, every delivery, every deal.

Remember: "Systems work, people fail."

But here's what most MSME founders experience instead:

- Daily chaos
- Endless fire-fighting
- Repeating the same instructions 10 times
- Micromanaging everything from procurement to payment
- A to-do list that never ends — even on Sundays

And after years of effort, they're left wondering:

"Why does my business still need *me* to run everything?"

Here's the truth:

You don't have a growth problem. You have a systems problem.

Your marketing may be working.

Leads may be coming.

Customers may be happy.

But if your backend is broken, everything will eventually hit a wall.

"You can't scale what isn't systemised. You can't relax in what isn't repeatable."

This chapter is your roadmap to escape daily chaos and take **strategic ownership.**

You'll learn how to build **systems that run the business — so you don't have to.**

Let's explore what's coming up.

The Problem: Founder Dependency = Growth Limiter

Most MSMEs are built like a tower of playing cards — with the founder at the base.

Every decision, client, invoice, and fire routes back to one person.

It feels noble in the beginning.

"I'll handle it myself."

"Nobody understands like I do."

"If I let go, quality will suffer."

But this founder-first model becomes your bottleneck.

You delay decisions.

Your team stops taking ownership.

Your business starts plateauing — not because of the market, but because of **capacity.**

The Agitation: Systems Seem Complicated, So We Avoid Them

Many MSME owners fear the word "systems."

They imagine:

- Expensive software
- Complicated SOPs
- Big teams
- Corporate-level bureaucracy
- Endless documentation

So they avoid it.

They keep running on gut feel, WhatsApp, reminders, and personal heroism.

But the cost is massive:

- Burnout
- Inconsistent service
- Missed opportunities
- Team confusion
- And zero scalability

The good news? **Systems don't have to be complicated. They have to be clear.**

This chapter gives you practical, MSME-friendly tools to start building your systems — one step at a time.

Let's look at the five powerful sections ahead.

Delegate Without Diluting Quality – Build Process, Not Dependence

Most MSMEs grow to a point — and then stall.

Why? Because the founder refuses (or fears) to delegate.

This section helps you:

- Identify what you *should* stop doing
- Create simple, repeatable processes (SOPs) for common tasks
- Train team members to deliver quality without needing hand-holding
- Use checklists and tools to reduce errors — even when you're not around

You'll stop being the bottleneck.

And your team will step up — with confidence and clarity.

Dashboards That Give You Clarity – Manage Through Data, Not Drama

Most founders spend their days asking:

- "Kitna maal nikla?"
- "Aaj ka collection kya hai?"
- "Client ne payment kiya ya nahi?"
- "Yeh order delay kyun ho gaya?"

You don't need more reports.

You need a **simple dashboard** that gives you the health of your business — in one glance.

This section teaches you how to:

- Track the 5–7 numbers that matter most
- Set up a Weekly Review Dashboard using Google Sheets or Notion
- Involve your team in updating it
- Use data to make fast, focused decisions

You'll shift from reactive to **strategic.**

Create Time Systems That Free You Up – Not Trap You Deeper

"I don't have time" is the #1 sentence MSME founders speak.

But the truth is — you don't have time because you don't have **time systems.**

This section helps you:

- Categorise your week into Focus, Flex, and Follow-up time
- Block thinking time, not just meeting time
- Design a weekly rhythm that balances growth, team, and operations
- Learn the Time Boxing Method used by high-performance entrepreneurs

Your calendar will stop being your enemy and become your **growth ally.**

Build a Self-Managed Team – Culture, Cadence & Accountability

Hiring is not enough. Managing is not enough.

What you need is a team that **self-manages**.

This section teaches you:

- How to set clear roles and KPIs
- How to run Weekly Accountability Meetings
- How to give feedback without conflict
- How to build a culture of initiative and ownership
- How to use scorecards and 1:1 check-ins to guide performance

You'll stop chasing people for updates.

Instead, your team will come to *you* with results and questions that matter.

Automate Without Overcomplicating – Use Tools That Save Time

The word "automation" often scares traditional MSMEs.

They imagine CRMs, ERPs, bots, workflows, and software costs.

But you don't need complex tools to simplify your life.

You need **smart, small automation** that frees up your team's time and reduces human error.

This section shows you the following:

- How to automate follow-ups using WhatsApp tools
- How to use CRMs like TeleCRM or LeadSquared for lead management
- How to send automated reports and reminders
- How to build no-code workflows with Google Sheets or free tools

You'll stop doing the same task 50 times — and start doing what actually moves the needle.

What You'll Gain from This Chapter

By the end of Chapter 6, you'll have:

☑ A delegation system that builds independence

☑ A dashboard that gives you real-time business health

☑ A time design that lets you focus on what matters

☑ A team rhythm that creates accountability

☑ An automation map that saves hours every week

This isn't just about scaling.

It's about **reclaiming your time.**

Your energy.

Your peace of mind.

It's about moving from **Founder-Operator → Founder-Leader.**

Turn the page — and let's start building systems that make your business *run like one*.

Delegate Without Diluting Quality:

If you're running an MSME and feel like you're working harder than ever — but still can't step away for even two days without something going wrong — you're not alone.

Every file needs your approval.

Every client wants to talk only to you.

Every small error ends up on your desk.

And your team? They're always "busy" but need you to think, check, approve, correct, remind.

Sound familiar?

It's not because your team is bad.

It's because your business is running on **people-dependence**, not **process-dependence**.

"If your business needs you to function — you don't own a business. You own a job."

This section is about shifting from founder-led chaos to **system-led consistency** — building **simple, powerful delegation structures** that free you up *without* compromising quality.

Let's fix the myth: Delegation is not losing control.

Delegation is **gaining time, trust, and traction.**

The Problem: The Founder as the Funnel

In most Indian MSMEs, the founder is the funnel.

Every decision passes through them, every task waits for their nod, and every problem lands on their WhatsApp at midnight.

Why? Because when the business was small, this worked.

But as orders grow, products expand, and clients multiply — the same style becomes a chokehold.

You can't scale decisions if you don't scale **responsibility**.

And that's where structured delegation comes in.

The Agitation: "I Can't Let Go — It'll Affect Quality"

Many founders resist delegation because of one fear:

"No one can do it like I do."

And to some extent — that's true.

But the question isn't, "Can they do it like you?"

The real question is: **Can they do it well enough, consistently, without bottlenecks?**

Because the real risk isn't delegation.

The real risk is **burnout**, bottlenecks, and lost opportunities because you're too busy fixing invoices while your competitors are closing deals.

Step 1: Identify What You *Must* Let Go

Not everything should be delegated.

But 70–80% of your weekly tasks **can** be.

Use the **Founder Time Audit**:

1.   For 5 days, write down everything you do — big and small.
2.   Categorise each task under:

Task Type	Delegate (D)	Automate (A)	Keep (K)
Client follow-up	D	A	
Invoice check	D		
Team hiring call			K
Vendor price compare	D		
Social media caption		A	

3. Anything that's low-value or repetitive — delegate or automate.

This audit becomes your first **delegation roadmap**.

Step 2: Build SOPs – Simple, Visual, and Actionable

SOP = Standard Operating Procedure

But don't get scared. It doesn't need to be a 20-page manual.

A good SOP is:

☑ Step-by-step

☑ Visual (screenshots/videos)

☑ Stored in one place (Google Drive/Notion/WhatsApp message)

☑ Easy to update

Example: **Client Onboarding SOP**

1. Welcome call within 24 hours
2. Send onboarding form (Google Form)
3. Add to CRM with notes
4. Schedule kick-off meeting
5. Send an invoice with standard terms
6. Confirm project start date

Tools to create SOPs:

- Google Docs for text
- Loom for video
- Canva for visual flowcharts
- Trello/ClickUp/Notion for tracking steps

Step 3: Delegate Outcomes, Not Just Tasks

Delegation is not: *"Print this file."*

Delegation is:

"Ensure client onboarding is complete within 2 days of payment. If any step is delayed, escalate to me."

When you delegate **tasks**, you stay involved.

When you delegate **outcomes**, your team takes ownership.

Give them:

- The goal
- The steps (SOP)
- The deadline
- The escalation paths
- The trust to execute

And then — *let them do it.*

Step 4: Train, Don't Just Tell

Many founders say, "I tried delegating. Didn't work."

But did you **train** — or just **tell**?

Training means:

- Walking them through the SOP live
- Letting them shadow you for 2–3 tasks
- Doing a mock run with feedback
- Let them do it while you observe

- Giving feedback till they hit consistency

It takes time in the beginning.

But saves **100X time** later.

Step 5: Use Tools That Help You Track Delegated Work

You don't need fancy dashboards.

Even a simple structure like this in Google Sheets or Trello works:

Task	Owner	Deadline	Status	Comments
Prepare a quote for Mr. Shah	Ramesh	12th Aug	In progress	Needs product list
Check GST returns	Preeti	15th Aug	Done	Submitted
Dispatch order #2381	Sanjay	11th Aug	Delayed	Courier issue

Review this in a **Weekly Team Huddle**.

No micromanagement. Just visibility.

"Delegation is not abdication. It's empowerment — backed by process and clarity."

Quick Self-Audit: Are You the Bottleneck?

☑ Do you answer more than 20 questions a day from your team?

☑ Do you spend time on ₹100 tasks as the founder?

☑ Do you fear taking 3 days off?

☑ Do clients insist on talking only to you?

☑ Do you check the same things over and over?

If yes — your next growth stage depends on **letting go smartly.**

Manage Through Data, Not Drama:

"Sir, the delivery scheduled for yesterday got delayed."

"Sir, the client has not cleared the payment yet."

"Sir, the rate confirmation from the vendor hasn't arrived."

"Sir, please confirm which invoice needs to be sent."

Sound familiar?

If you're a founder constantly being interrupted by updates, status checks, and decisions, you're not managing a business; you're **managing noise**.

The solution?

A clear, simple, visible system that tells you **exactly what's happening** in your business — without you having to ask every time.

That system is called a **Dashboard.**

"Without a dashboard, you're driving blind. With one, you lead with insight."

This section is about helping you build a **real-time, weekly updated business dashboard** that brings you clarity, speed, and control without complexity or expensive tools.

The Problem: MSME Founders Run on Gut-Feel, Not Visibility

Most founders make decisions based on the following:

- What they remember
- What their team tells them
- What the gut says
- Or what feels urgent

This style may have worked when the business was small.

But as your team grows, orders increase, cash flow gets tighter, and marketing expands — **you need numbers, not noise.**

Here's what happens without a dashboard:

- You chase updates from 5 different people
- Your team forgets to inform you until it's too late
- You miss red flags
- You can't spot trends
- You react instead of planning

You feel **busy** — but not in control.

The Agitation: More Reports Don't Help — Simpler Ones Do

Some MSMEs try to fix this by creating endless Excel files.

One for sales, One for payments, One for stock, One for tasks, One for marketing, One that nobody opens again, And every week, you ask your team, *"Update kiya kya?"*

This doesn't work. Why?

- Too many files
- No single source of truth

- No habit of reviewing regularly
- No decisions coming out of the data

The result? Frustration and confusion.

The solution? **One Dashboard. Updated weekly, used daily.**

Step 1: Choose the Right Format (Use What Your Team Can Handle)

Don't chase ERP software or paid tools unless you need them.

Start with what your team already uses.

Best MSME-friendly dashboard tools:

- ☑ Google Sheets (free, collaborative, real-time)

- ☑ Trello or ClickUp (for task tracking + dashboard views)

- ☑ WhatsApp Weekly Reports (in early stages)

If your team is not digitally strong, even a **whiteboard with markers** in the office works—as long as it is updated **every Friday.**

Step 2: Decide the Core Areas You Want to Monitor

A founder's dashboard does **not** have about 50 metrics.

About **7–10 key numbers** tell you how your business is doing.

Suggested Dashboard Sections:

Category	Metrics (Examples)
Sales & Revenue	Orders this week, Invoiced amount
Payments & Cash	Collections done, Pending receivables
Operations	Orders delivered, Delays, Complaints
Marketing	Leads generated, CPL, ROAS
Inventory (if applicable)	Stock alerts, Low-quantity items
Team Accountability	Tasks due, Tasks completed, Escalations
Customer Experience	NPS score, Reviews, Refunds

Pick what applies to your business. Don't overcomplicate.

Step 3: Assign Ownership – Who Updates What?

The dashboard won't update itself.

So, create a system:

Metric	Owner	Update Frequency
Orders This Week	Sales Lead	Every Friday
Pending Payments	Accounts	Every Friday
Leads This Week	Marketing	Every Friday
Tasks Completed	Team Leads	Every Friday

Make it part of your **Weekly Ritual**.

Every Friday, 4–5 people update their section by 4 PM.

Saturday morning: The founder reviews it with the team for 30 minutes.

This habit builds rhythm, clarity, and accountability.

Step 4: Use Traffic Light Indicators

Don't just see numbers. **See health.**

Colour-code your metrics:

- ☑ **Green** – On track
- ◯ **Yellow** – Slight delay or warning
- ⬤ **Red** – Immediate attention needed

Examples:

Metric	Target	Actual	Status
Leads This Week	50	58	☑
Orders Delivered	30	21	⬤
Collection %	80%	74%	◯

This makes your review **fast and focused**.

No scrolling through 12 tabs. Just decisions.

Step 5: Use the Dashboard to Make Weekly Decisions

Your dashboard is not just for display.

It must answer:

- What's working? → Double down
- What's not working? → Fix it
- Who's stuck? → Support them
- What's improving? → Celebrate it
- What's risky? → Prevent it

This is how your **team starts solving problems — not just escalating them.**

And you? You stop micro-managing and start **leading.**

Bonus Tip: Create a Founder Snapshot Page

Have one top sheet that gives you a quick view:

WEEKLY FOUNDER SNAPSHOT

- Total Sales: ₹2,40,000
- New Leads: 78
- Collections: ₹1,60,000
- Orders Delivered: 33
- Team Tasks Overdue: 5
- Complaints: 2
- Growth Highlight: Closed biggest corporate order (₹80K)
- Risk Highlight: Dispatch delay in East zone

One page. 3-minute read. 360° control.

Quick Self-Check: Do You Have Dashboard Clarity?

☑ Do you know your sales for this week — without asking three people?

☑ Do you know which team is lagging?

☑ Do you know your CPL or ROAS from the last campaign?

☑ Do you track weekly collections vs targets?

☑ Do you have one place where all this lives?

If not — now is the time.

Create Time Systems That Free You Up:

Ask any MSME founder what they want more of, and the answer is almost always the same:

"Time."

Time to think, Time to plan, Time to breathe, Time to spend with family, Time to grow the business — instead of just running after daily tasks.

But here's the irony: Most founders have filled their calendars to the brim, yet they feel they're always behind.

Meetings run late.

Calls come unplanned.

Important tasks get missed.

At the end of the day, you're exhausted but unsure of what really moved the business forward.

"You don't need more hours. You need a better system for the hours you already have."

This section will show you how to create **founder-friendly time systems** that protect your focus, give your day structure, and make space for real growth work — not just urgent work.

Let's start.

The Problem: Busy but Not Productive

Most MSME founders live in a constant state of **reaction**.

• A vendor calls — you pick up.

• A team member is confused — you drop everything to help.

• A WhatsApp message pings — you respond.

• A customer delays payment — you chase it personally.

• A family member reminds you about a missed commitment — you feel guilty.

It's a loop.

You're always on. Always accessible. Always involved.

But rarely *in control*.

You confuse motion with progress.

The Agitation: Lack of Time Systems Leads to Founder Fatigue

This kind of reactive work-life leads to:

- Poor decision-making
- No strategic thinking time
- Dropped commitments
- Constant distractions
- Burnout masked as "hustle"

You feel guilty when you're not working.

But even guiltier when you are — because the work never ends.

The truth is that your business doesn't need **more of you**.

It needs **a better version of you** — one who is focused, energetic, and thinking three steps ahead.

That's only possible if you create **time systems that protect your bandwidth.**

Step 1: Block Your Time Like a CEO, Not a Worker

Start by dividing your work week into **three zones**:

Zone	Purpose	Example Activities
Focus Time	Deep work that grows the business	Strategy, Product development, Writing SOPs
Flex Time	Collaborative time	Team calls, Client meetings, Vendor discussions
Follow-Up Time	Admin, approvals, quick fixes	WhatsApp replies, Checking reports, Email responses

Now, assign time blocks to each category across the week.

Example Weekly Template:

Day	9–12 PM	12–2 PM	3–5 PM	5–6 PM
Monday	Focus (Product)	Flex (Team)	Focus (Leads)	Follow-Up
Tuesday	Focus (Strategy)	Flex (Clients)	Flex (Vendor)	Follow-Up
Wednesday	Flex (Team)	Focus (Writing SOPs)	Focus (Review)	Follow-Up

Protect your **Focus Time** like your life depends on it because it does — at least the life of your next growth stage.

Step 2: Use the Time Boxing Method

Don't create a vague to-do list.

Instead, **assign each task to a specific time block**.

Example:

- ☑ "Reply to vendor quotes" → 11:00–11:30 AM
- ☑ "Review social media calendar" → 2:00–2:45 PM
- ☑ "Call Mr. Tiwari for feedback" → 4:15–4:30 PM

This eliminates:

- Task overlap
- Endless postponing
- Overbooking
- Decision fatigue

You stop asking, *"What should I do next?"*

You start knowing, *"Here's what's next — and for how long."*

Step 3: Set Meeting Boundaries

Meetings are productivity killers **if unstructured.**

Set clear rules:

- No meetings longer than 45 minutes unless critical
- Every meeting must have an agenda sent in advance
- Default mode: Weekly sync-ups, not daily check-ins

- Use shared documents (like Google Docs/Sheets) for updates — no need to repeat everything verbally

Train your team to solve, escalate only when needed, and **respect your calendar.**

Step 4: Use a Weekly Founder Planner

Create a recurring Sunday evening or Monday morning ritual:

Your 30-minute Weekly Reset

☑ Review what happened last week

☑ See what got missed

☑ Pick 3–5 priorities for the upcoming week

☑ Time-box those into your calendar

☑ Flag potential bottlenecks

☑ Share the plan with your core team

Tools: Google Calendar, Notion, Trello, or even a notebook — just be consistent.

This creates **clarity for your brain and direction for your team.**

Step 5: Design Your "Unbreakable" Power Hours

Every founder needs **non-negotiable weekly windows**—no meetings, calls, or WhatsApp distractions are allowed.

Call it your "CEO Window."

Maybe it's:

- 8:30–10:00 AM daily
- 2:00–4:00 PM on Tue/Thu
- Sunday 10–12 noon at a café

In this window, you only work *on* the business — not *in* it.

Use it to: Think, Write, Plan, Build, Review and Learn

These hours may only be 6–8 per week.

But they are worth more than 60 scattered ones.

Bonus: Audit Your Distractions

Keep a "Distraction Tracker" for 3 days.

Every time you're interrupted, note:

- Time
- What interrupted you
- Was it urgent?
- Can it be eliminated or delegated?

You'll discover shocking patterns.

From there, you can create:

☑ WhatsApp mute zones

☑ No-meeting half-days

☑ Delegation triggers

☑ Assistant filters for unimportant stuff

You'll gain **hours back** — every week.

Quick Self-Check: Are You Owning Your Time?

☑ Do you have at least 5–8 hours of Focus Time weekly?

☑ Do you know your top 3 business priorities each week?

☑ Do you start each day with a time-boxed calendar?

☑ Does your team respect your availability rules?

☑ Do you spend time on growth — not just operations?

If not — your time is running out.

It's time to flip that.

Build a Self-Managed Team:

You've heard the phrase:

"If you want to go fast, go alone. If you want to go far, go together."

But for most MSME founders, going together often feels like a drag — not a boost.

You find yourself:

- Chasing your team for updates
- Repeating the same instructions
- Solving the same problems
- Putting out fires they should've handled
- Wondering if hiring even helped at all

It's exhausting.

And you start thinking, *"It's faster if I do it myself."*

But that mindset traps you in **permanent operator mode** — where you're always needed to *run* the business but never free to *grow* it.

"You don't just need a bigger team. You need a team that thinks, acts, and grows with you."

This section is about building a **self-managed team** that takes ownership, solves problems, and delivers results *without constant hand-holding*.

Let's make that possible.

The Problem: Most Teams Are Busy and not Accountable

Here's what happens in most MSMEs:

- People show up. They stay busy.
- But goals are vague. Roles are fuzzy.
- Meetings are irregular. Follow-ups are informal.
- There are no clear metrics for success.
- Founders stay involved in everything.

So, the team waits. They escalate. They depend.

They work — but without clarity or cadence.

This isn't a team problem. It's a **system problem.**

The Agitation: Founder-First Culture Limits Growth

When everything flows through you...

- Decisions slow down
- Team confidence stays low
- Mistakes repeat
- You become a bottleneck
- Growth hits a ceiling

And worst of all — you get tired of managing people.

Not because people are the problem. But because **the structure is missing.**

Your team doesn't need more pressure.

They need a **system of ownership.**

Step 1: Define Clear Roles and Outcomes

People don't take ownership when:

- They're not sure what they *own*
- Their tasks change every day
- There's no clarity on how success is measured

Start with this:

Role	Key Responsibility	Success Metrics
Sales Lead	Convert inbound leads	Weekly leads, conversion rate
Ops Manager	Timely order delivery	% on-time, client complaints
Accounts	Collections and payout tracking	DSO (Days Sales Outstanding), Accuracy
Social Media	Content and engagement	Followers, Reach, Lead Inquiries

Each person should own 2–3 clear metrics.

Not just tasks — **outcomes.**

Now, instead of asking: *"Tumne kya kiya?"*

You'll ask: *"Where are we on your weekly metric?"*

That's the shift.

Step 2: Establish a Weekly Rhythm

You don't need daily check-ins.

You need **weekly clarity.**

Create a weekly cadence:

- **Monday Morning**: Team Huddle (30 mins)
    - What's the top priority this week?
    - Any bottlenecks?
    - Metric updates
    - Who owns what?
- **Mid-Week Check-in (Optional)**: Quick progress sync
- **Friday Wrap-Up**: Each team member sends:
    - What they completed
    - Any delays + reason
    - What they'll improve next week

Tools to manage this:

- Google Sheets
- WhatsApp formatted updates
- Trello, ClickUp, or Notion
- Voice notes if the team isn't tech-savvy

This rhythm builds **momentum + ownership.**

Step 3: Use Scorecards for Performance Tracking

You can't manage what you don't measure.

And you can't grow what you don't review.

Create a **Monthly Team Scorecard**:

Team Member	Role	Metrics	Target	Actual	Comments
Ramesh	Sales Lead	Conversion Rate	20%	17%	Lost one key deal
Asha	Dispatch	On-Time Orders	95%	96%	Excellent recovery
Preeti	Accounts	Collection Rate	90%	82%	Delay in 3 clients

Review this **once a month**.

Praise performance. Coach where needed.

Make it a **two-way dialogue**, not a one-sided grilling.

Step 4: Conduct Monthly 1:1 Conversations

Big problems often hide in silence. Your team needs space to:

- Share what's blocking them
- Ask for support
- Suggest improvements
- Feel heard and appreciated

Do a **monthly 15–20 minute 1:1 call** with each team member.

Ask:

☑ What's working well for you right now?

☑ What's one thing that's frustrating you?

☑ How can I support you better?

☑ What's one area you'd like to grow in?

These 1:1s build **trust + retention + performance**.

Step 5: Build a Culture of Ownership, Not Obedience

Ownership grows when your team:

- It feels safe to speak up
- Is clear on what success looks like
- Is recognised for results
- Gets feedback regularly
- Sees their ideas get implemented

Simple ways to reinforce this:

☑ Start a "Win of the Week" moment in Monday huddles

☑ Allow team members to lead small projects

☑ Celebrate small wins — publicly

☑ Let the team present weekly numbers — not you

☑ Say "thank you" more often — with specifics

This creates a **culture that performs even when you're not watching.**

Quick Self-Check: Do You Have a Self-Managed Team?

☑ Do your team members have clearly defined roles and metrics?

☑ Do you have a weekly review rhythm in place?

☑ Are outcomes tracked, not just activities?

☑ Do your team members solve problems before escalating?

☑ Are you spending less time in "reminder mode" and more time in "review mode"?

If not — it's time to shift from people pressure to **people process.**

Automate Without Overcomplicating:

Let's be honest.

When MSME founders hear the word "automation," two things usually happen:

- Either they feel intimidated: *"We're too small for that tech stuff."*
- Or they imagine huge costs: *"ERP? CRM? AI bots? That's for the big players."*

But here's the truth:

You don't need fancy tech. You need smart systems.

Systems that reduce manual work.

Systems that ensure follow-ups happen — even when you forget.

Systems that minimise human error, save time and give your team more bandwidth.

"Automation is not about replacing people. It's about freeing them to do better work."

In this chapter, we'll show you how to use **simple, practical automation** to reduce repetitive tasks, improve accuracy, and let your business run smoother — *without making it robotic.*

Let's build your automation muscle — without breaking your budget or your brain.

The Problem: Manual Everything = Mistakes + Missed Growth

Let's look at how most MSMEs operate:

- Leads come from WhatsApp, Facebook, calls — all over the place
- Follow-ups are manual (or forgotten)
- Quotes are sent manually every time
- Customer data is scattered across notebooks, Excel sheets, and team members' phones
- Reports are made at the last minute — or not at all
- Reminders? Only when someone remembers

This isn't just inefficient.

It leads to:

- Lost leads
- Delayed payments
- Poor customer experience
- Frustrated teams
- No scalability

Your people are busy — but the business isn't growing *smart*.

The Agitation: Fear of Tools = Staying Stuck

Many founders avoid automation because of three myths:

- **"I'm not tech-savvy."**
- **"My team can't handle new software."**
- **"This will take too much time to set up."**

But here's the reality:

You can automate it if you use WhatsApp, email, or Excel.

And your team doesn't need to learn coding or software. They need **systems designed for real users.**

You don't need more complexity.

You need **clarity + consistency + control.** Automation delivers all three.

Step 1: Automate Your Lead Capture & Follow-Up

Let's start with the **easiest win**—lead follow-up.

Current Problem:

A lead comes via Instagram DM. You forward it to the sales guy. He says, "Noted." Then forgets.

Solution:

Use a basic CRM like **TeleCRM** or **LeadSquared** or a shared **Google Sheet + WhatsApp automation tool** like WA Sender.

How it works:

- Every lead gets added to one central CRM
- You set follow-up dates and reminders
- A WhatsApp welcome message or email goes instantly
- The system pings the sales team until action is taken

- Follow-ups are tracked automatically

This ensures **zero leakages**, **faster response**, and **better conversion.**

Even if your sales rep changes — the data stays.

Step 2: Use WhatsApp for Smart Automation (Your Customers Already Are)

WhatsApp is your customer's preferred platform.

So use it to:

- Send **order confirmations**
- Share **payment links or reminders**
- Send **support tickets or queries**
- Share **automated feedback forms**
- Run **weekly broadcast updates**

Tools like **WA Web Plus, DoubleTick,** or **WA Sender Pro** help you:

- Schedule messages
- Create follow-up sequences
- Personalise bulk messages (Name + Order ID)
- Tag and segment customers (hot leads, repeat clients, etc.)

No website is needed, no coding is required—just smart usage of an app you're already using.

Step 3: Create Auto-Reports with Google Sheets

You don't need software to get insights.

You can turn a basic Google Sheet into a **live dashboard** with:

- Auto-updated sales totals
- Daily order summaries
- Weekly collection reports
- Colour-coded performance trackers

Add simple formulas + conditional formatting.

Use filters. Link multiple tabs.

Use tools like **Google Forms** to collect team updates and connect them to Sheets. Now, you don't need to chase numbers. They appear **on their own.**

Step 4: Automate Repetitive Documents & Emails

Are you typing the same quotation again and again?

Create templates in:

- **Google Docs** for quotes, emails, delivery notes
- **Excel** for invoice generation
- **Canva** for repeat creatives
- **Gmail Canned Responses** for frequently sent messages

You can even use tools like **Zapier** or **Make.com** to trigger:

- A thank-you email when a form is filled
- A task in Trello when a lead is added
- A Google Calendar reminder when payment is due

These are small automations. But together, they save **hours per week.**

Step 5: Start Small, Scale Slowly

You don't have to automate everything on Day 1.

Start with just 2–3 systems:

- ☑ Lead tracking + follow-up CRM

- ☑ WhatsApp automation for repeat updates

- ☑ Google Sheet for auto-reporting

Once your team is comfortable, add more.

Remember: **adoption beats ambition.**

Fancy tools mean nothing if your team doesn't use them.

Choose **low-friction, high-clarity tools** that integrate with your current habits.

"Automation is not a luxury. It's a survival tool — especially when you're scaling."

Bonus: Map Your Automation Opportunities

Use this table to plan what to automate next:

Area	Current Manual Process	Tool/Automation to Try
Lead Follow-Up	WhatsApp messages manually	TeleCRM, WA Sender
Quotation	Word file created from scratch	Google Docs Template
Payment Reminder	Manual follow-up on calls	WhatsApp Broadcast with WA Pro
Order Status	Team calls to update	Google Sheets + shared tracker
Daily Reports	Sent via WhatsApp messages	Google Form + Sheet dashboard

Even saving **10 minutes per task** leads to **5+ hours per week.**

That's not automation. That's **liberation.**

Chapter 7: High-Ownership Team Culture

Your systems are improving.

You've structured your time, created dashboards and automated tasks, and your team performs better.

But despite all of this, something still feels missing.

That spark. That initiative. That *emotional ownership*.

You walk into your business, and you don't feel energy.

You don't feel passion.

You don't feel like your team *cares* as much as you do.

They do the job.

But not with the heart, urgency, or commitment you'd hoped for.

"The real difference between a good team and a great one isn't skills — it's culture."

This chapter is not about systems, tools, or automation.

It's about something deeper and more powerful — **team culture**.

Because without a strong culture, your business will always feel like a machine that needs constant oiling.

But with the right culture, your business becomes **a self-sustaining ecosystem** where people care, improve, and grow *independently*.

Let's build that kind of team.

The Problem: Skill Without Culture = Mediocrity

Most MSMEs focus only on hiring for skills.

Can they manage accounts?

Can they deliver orders?

Can they follow the SOP?

And while technical skills are essential, they're not enough.

You might hire a capable person — but still find them:

- Avoiding responsibility
- Blaming others for errors
- Escaping tough conversations
- Saying, "This isn't my job."
- Clocking out mentally, even if they're physically present

This is not a skill issue. It's a **culture issue**.

A weak culture drains energy, kills ownership, and turns even talented employees into disengaged workers.

The Agitation: Without Culture, Systems Collapse Under Pressure

Even the best SOPs and dashboards won't save you if the mindset is broken.

When the team doesn't feel:

- Safe to speak up
- Encouraged to improve
- Responsible for results
- Proud of their work
- Connected to a shared purpose

Then things slowly start slipping.

You, as the founder, feel like:

- You always have to remind people
- Initiative is rare
- Feedback is taken personally
- Good people leave quietly
- Your energy is spent managing people, not leading them

This is emotional fatigue.

It's cultural erosion.

And left unaddressed, it **kills long-term growth**.

The Solution: Build a Culture of Ownership, Not Obedience

This chapter will show you how to build a **deliberate, high-ownership culture** where:

- People take the initiative without waiting
- Mistakes are treated as learning moments
- Feedback is welcomed, not feared
- Wins are shared, celebrated, and repeated
- The team doesn't just work for salary — they work for pride

This culture doesn't require a big office, a fancy HR department, or expensive retreats.

It requires **clarity, consistency, and care.**

Let's walk through the five foundational pillars we'll cover next.

The Culture Gap: Why Most Teams Just Do the Job

In this section, we uncover the **root causes** of low team energy.

You'll learn:

- Why do people "check out" mentally, even if they show up physically
- The difference between a *task culture* and an *ownership culture*
- How small behaviour patterns destroy long-term accountability

> - Real stories from Indian MSMEs where culture shifted everything

This section opens your eyes to the *real cost* of poor culture — and how it silently blocks scale, sales, and sanity.

Culture by Design – Not by Default

Culture is being created in your business — whether you know it or not.

This section helps you move from *accidental* to *intentional* culture-building.

You'll learn how to:

- Define your team values clearly
- Create a "Culture Canvas" — your internal playbook
- Align hiring, onboarding, and recognition with values
- Replace vague expectations with clear behaviours

Because strong cultures aren't built in workshops.

They're built-in **daily decisions**.

Create Your Culture Operating System – Rituals, Rhythms, Reinforcement

This section gives you the **systems behind the culture.**

For example, if you have a sales process or delivery SOP, you need a **culture process.**

We'll show you:

- Daily, weekly, and monthly rituals that build team unity
- Recognition frameworks (without spending much)
- How to build feedback loops that don't create fear
- What to say and do when values are violated

You'll generate a **structure for soft things** — and that's the secret to a culture that lasts.

Daily Leadership Habits for Founders – Set the Tone

Culture starts at the top. Always.

This section is for *you*, the founder.

You'll learn:

- How to model the behaviours you want your team to adopt
- How to correct without crushing
- How to praise publicly and coach privately
- How to stay emotionally regulated when things go wrong
- How to build trust that's *earned*, not enforced

Because your habits shape the team more than any rulebook ever will.

Accountability Without Micromanagement

Accountability is often misunderstood.

Too much control? People feel suffocated.

Too much freedom? People become careless.

This section teaches you the **balance**:

- Set expectations that are clear, not vague
- Use scorecards to track progress without chasing
- Hold 1:1s that drive performance without pressure
- Create a culture where team members hold *each other* accountable

This is the final bridge between culture and execution — where ownership becomes **automatic.**

Why Most Teams Just 'Do the Job':

Walk into any average MSME office or workshop, and you'll find people who are:

- Showing up on time
- Completing assigned tasks
- Following instructions
- Delivering output

But here's what you *won't* always find:

- Energy
- Initiative
- Passion
- Ownership
- Innovation

The team is "working" — but they're not **engaged**.

They're doing the job, not **driving the business**.

"A culture of compliance creates survival. A culture of ownership creates scale."

This section unpacks the *silent killer* of growth in MSMEs—the **culture gap**—and helps you see why your team might be stuck in 'task mode' rather than rising to its true potential.

The Problem: Work Is Getting Done... But Growth Isn't

On the surface, your team may seem fine.

Orders are going out.

Accounts are managed.

Leads are being followed up.

But beneath the surface, here's what's likely happening:

- People avoid responsibility for mistakes
- Deadlines are met but with minimal effort
- Feedback is taken personally, not professionally
- Ideas are rare, and risks are avoided
- Performance depends on pressure — not passion

It feels like **you are the engine**, and the team is just getting pulled along.

They don't act like business builders.

They act like **salary-seekers**.

And over time, you feel tired, disappointed, or even *trapped*.

The Agitation: Without Ownership, Everything Requires Your Push

Here's how the culture gap shows up:

- You can't take a 3-day break without worrying
- You end up double-checking every task
- You're constantly reminding people of what's already been said
- Good team members leave, saying: *"I don't see a future here."*
- You hesitate to grow because you don't trust the team can handle it

And this isn't about skill or salary.

It's about **mindset and environment.**

Even the most capable team members will eventually check out mentally if the culture does not support them:

- Trust
- Growth
- Recognition
- Psychological safety
- Shared goals

This is the **invisible barrier** to scaling — and most MSMEs don't even know it exists until it's too late.

Story: The Two Shops on the Same Lane

Let's look at a real-world contrast.

There are two mobile repair shops on the same street in Surat.

Shop A:

The owner arrives every day at 10:30 AM. The team waits for instructions. No one makes decisions on their own. If customers complain, they say, "Wait till sir comes." Staff turnover is high. The team "follows orders" but doesn't care beyond the clock.

Shop B:

The founder isn't always present, but the team knows its roles. It greets customers, offers solutions, and makes decisions. It's even created a shared "knowledge doc" to train new staff.

Customers return often—not just for service but for the **experience**.

Same location. Same market.

But a different outcome — because of **culture**.

What Causes the Culture Gap?

Most MSMEs don't *create* culture.

They let it **happen by default.**

Here's what typically leads to a disengaged team:

1. No Shared Vision

The team doesn't know why the business exists beyond "making money."

2. No Clear Values

There's no understanding of *how* things should be done — only what needs to be done.

3. No Recognition

Effort goes unnoticed. Only errors get attention. So, people stop trying.

4. Fear-Based Environment

Mistakes are punished. Opinions are risky. So, people keep their heads down.

5. Inconsistent Leadership

The founder's mood defines the day — not the mission. There's no emotional consistency.

These gaps don't appear overnight.

They build over time — silently corroding trust, performance, and morale.

The Solution: Recognise That Culture Is a System

Culture is not about:

- Birthday parties
- T-shirts with logos
- Fancy quotes on walls

Culture is about:

- The **behaviours you reward**
- The **mistakes you tolerate**
- The **conversations you allow**
- The **trust you build**
- The **standards you uphold**

And like any business system — culture can be **designed, documented, and improved.**

Quick Audit: Do You Have a Culture Gap?

Ask yourself:

☑ Do team members take the initiative without being told?

☑ Do they care about the outcome — or just task completion?

☑ Are ideas coming from them — or only from you?

☑ Are tough conversations avoided or handled well?

☑ Do people feel proud to say they work with you?

If most of your answers are NO — it's not a people problem.

It's a **culture problem.**

And the good news is — culture can be built.

Culture by Design Not by Default:

Culture is not created in boardrooms or written on walls.

It is created in the **small, daily behaviours** that your team sees, feels, and follows.

- How your team talks to each other
- How leaders respond to mistakes
- Who gets appreciated (and who doesn't)
- What is tolerated (and what is not)
- How decisions are made under pressure

"Whether you build it or not, culture is forming in your business — every single day."

So the question is not, *"Do we have a culture?"*

The real question is: **"Is our culture helping us grow — or holding us back?"**

This section is about deliberately building your team culture.

Not as an emotional concept but a practical, systemised, and leadership-driven framework that shapes how your people behave when no one is watching.

The Problem: Accidental culture = Inconsistent Behaviour

Let's say you haven't defined your team values.

What happens?

- Every team member has their interpretation of what's "okay."
- Decisions vary depending on who's in charge that day
- New hires learn from the loudest voices — not the best examples
- Accountability is patchy, and bias creeps in
- Energy and performance fluctuate based on mood, not mission

This creates confusion, misalignment, and long-term cracks in your organisation's foundation.

And in a growing MSME, **every crack leaks culture.**

The Agitation: No Culture System = Founder Frustration

Have you ever thought:

- "Why don't they think like owners?"
- "Why is everyone waiting for me to say what to do?"
- "Why is there so much drama in the team?"
- "Why is nobody taking initiative unless I'm watching?"

These are signs that your culture is driven by **default**, not **design**.

And without a designed culture, your growth will always rely on your **presence** instead of your **principles**.

It's time to fix that.

Step 1: Define the Core Values That Guide Your Business

Core values are not motivational posters.

They are **decision-making tools**.

They help your team answer the following:

- What does good behaviour look like here?
- What do we reward? What do we reject?
- How do we treat each other, clients, and vendors?

Start by identifying 3–5 values that reflect your highest expectations.

Avoid generic words like "Integrity" or "Excellence." Make them **real, specific, and action-driven.**

Examples:

Value	Description
Own the Outcome	We don't blame. We solve and deliver results.
Speak with Respect	We give feedback honestly — but never with ego or insults.
Learn, Don't Repeat	Mistakes are okay — repeating them is not.
Keep it Simple	Don't overcomplicate. Clarity is better than cleverness.
Client First, Always	We act in the client's best interest — even under pressure.

Display these values. Talk about them. Hire, fire, promote, and reward **based on them.**

Step 2: Build Your Culture Canvas

The **Culture Canvas** is a simple one-page guide that explains:

1. **Our Purpose** – Why we do what we do
2. **Our Core Values** – The behaviours we expect
3. **Our team Promises** – What each team member commits to
4. **Our Rituals** – How we reinforce culture (meetings, recognition, feedback, etc.)
5. **What We Don't Tolerate** – Non-negotiables (e.g., gossip, excuses, disrespect)

Use a tool like Canva or Notion to build it visually. Print and share it with every team member.

This becomes your **internal compass** — for new hires, daily work, and crisis moments.

Step 3: Align Hiring and Onboarding with Culture

Don't wait till someone joins to check cultural fit.

Instead:

☑ Ask cultural-fit questions during interviews.

☑ Share the Culture Canvas before they join.

☑ During onboarding, explain each value with real examples.

☑ Assign a team buddy to demonstrate expected behaviour.

Remember: **skills can be trained, but values must align.**

If someone's attitude doesn't match your culture, no amount of talent will compensate for the damage they cause.

Step 4: Turn Values into Daily Practice

Culture isn't built in one session.

It's built-in **repetition**.

Ideas to bring your values alive daily:

- Start meetings with a "Culture Check" — e.g., "Who showed 'Own the Outcome' this week?"
- Highlight team wins by linking them to values
- Use a whiteboard/Slack group to celebrate "Value Champions."
- Have monthly peer-nominated recognitions for best culture contributor
- When correcting behaviour, refer to the value — not personal attack

For example, "This feels like a break in 'Speak with Respect' — let's fix that."

The more often values are spoken, seen, and celebrated — the more they stick.

Step 5: Protect the Culture — Ruthlessly

Your job as the founder is not just to build the culture.

Your job is to **protect it fiercely.**

That means:

- Firing fast when someone violates values repeatedly
- Calling out drama, gossip, and blame
- Being consistent — even when it's uncomfortable
- Being the first to apologise if *you* break a value

Your team is watching.

And culture isn't what you say.

It's what you **allow**.

Quick Self-Check: Are You Building Culture by Design?

☑ Have you clearly defined 3–5 core values with your team?

☑ Do you talk about them in meetings and onboarding?

☑ Are you rewarding behaviour that matches your values?

☑ Is there a one-page Culture Canvas everyone can see?

☑ Do you take action when values are broken?

If not — it's time to move from accidental to intentional.

Create Your Culture Operating System:

A high-performing team culture isn't built through motivational speeches or one-time workshops.

It's built through **repetition**.

Through **daily behaviours**, **weekly rhythms**, and **monthly reflections**.

Just like a computer runs on an operating system, your business culture also needs an **OS**—something that doesn't depend on mood, memory, or management pressure.

"Culture becomes real when it becomes routine."

In this section, we'll help you design your **Culture Operating System** — a set of **rituals, rhythms, and reinforcement habits** that keep your team aligned, energised, and accountable without needing your daily intervention.

Let's turn your culture from a concept into a **working system**.

The Problem: Culture Without Rhythm Fades Fast

You might have defined your values.

You may have created a beautiful Culture Canvas.

But unless it is lived and reinforced **consistently**, it fades.

Here's what usually happens in MSMEs:

- Culture is discussed during onboarding... and never again
- Core values are written on the wall but not linked to decisions
- Recognition happens randomly — only when a crisis is avoided
- Feedback is delayed or avoided altogether
- Conversations are either too formal (monthly reviews) or too casual (WhatsApp rants)

This inconsistency creates confusion.

And culture thrives on **clarity + consistency**.

Without a regular rhythm, culture becomes a *poster*, not a *practice*.

The Agitation: Without Systems, Culture Feels Like Effort

You can't keep manually:

- Reminding people about values
- Chasing teams for updates
- Praising good behaviour only when you remember
- Repeating the same feedback every month

It's exhausting.

Worse, your team starts thinking: *"The Founder's mood decides the culture."*

That's the death of ownership.

To grow, you need a **self-reinforcing loop** in which culture takes care of itself through **rituals, systems, and peer involvement**.

Let's design that now.

Step 1: Install Daily & Weekly Team Rituals

Rituals are simple, short, structured actions that anchor your team in shared values and goals.

They create rhythm and reinforce identity.

⬤ **Daily Rituals**

1. Morning Stand-Up (10–15 mins):

- Each person shares:
    - What they did yesterday
    - What they're doing today
    - Any blockers

Optional add-on: End the stand-up with one team member giving a quick shout-out to a colleague who displayed a core value.

2. Start-of-Shift Check-ins:

- Especially for factory/shop floor teams
- 5-minute circle: quick brief, safety check, daily goal

3. "Value of the Day" Reminder:

- Rotate one core value each day
- Send a short WhatsApp message or display it on the office whiteboard

- Ask: *"Where can we apply this today?"*

⬤ **Weekly Rituals**

1. Monday Morning Huddle (30 mins):

- Review key numbers (Sales, Leads, Deliveries)
- Highlight 1–2 value-driven wins
- Share the top 3 focus areas for the week
- Assign clear outcomes and owners

2. Friday Wins & Learnings (30 mins):

- Team members share:
  - Biggest win of the week
  - What didn't go well and what they learned
  - Who deserves a "value shoutout."

These two meetings create a **bookend effect** — alignment at the start and reflection at the end.

Step 2: Build a Recognition Framework (Without Needing Big Budgets)

Recognition is **the cheapest and most powerful fuel** for a high-performance culture.

But it must be structured.

System 1: The "Value Champion" of the Week

- Every Friday, the team nominates a colleague who best lives a core value

- Display their photo + the story behind the recognition
- Small reward: a handwritten note, spotlight in WhatsApp group, or ₹200 food voucher

System 2: Peer-to-Peer Praise Board

- A whiteboard or Notion page where anyone can write:
  - "Thank you to [Name] for helping with [Task] — showed [Value] beautifully."

System 3: Random Acts of Appreciation

- Founder or team leads give "surprise thanks" via voice, email, or sticky notes.
- Recognise *effort*, not just results

Recognition turns abstract values into **visible, emotional experiences**.

Step 3: Build a Feedback Rhythm

Feedback shouldn't be feared.

It should be expected.

But that only happens when it's regular, respectful, and linked to growth.

🔁 Monthly 1-on-1 Feedback Loop

Every team member gets a 20-minute feedback conversation covering:

- What they're doing well (tie to a value)
- What needs to improve (tie to a value)
- What support do they need
- What goal they're aiming for next month

Golden Rule: Praise publicly, correct privately.

Create a simple 1:1 Tracker in Google Sheets:

Team Member	Praise	Growth Area	Next Goal	Support Needed
Asha	Great client rapport	Clarity in reports	Submit weekly report on time	Time audit template

This loop builds **trust, clarity, and performance**.

Step 4: Add Monthly Culture Review to Your Calendar

Once a month, the leadership team should ask:

- Are our rituals being followed?
- Which value is being lived the most?
- Which value is being ignored?
- Is any toxicity/gossip creeping in?
- Who deserves a leadership opportunity?

Use these insights to evolve and reinforce your Culture OS.

"Systems don't kill culture. Systems sustain it."

The more automated your culture rituals become, the more your team adopts and protects them — even when you're not around.

Quick Self-Check: Do You Have a Culture OS?

☑ Do you have daily/weekly team rituals?

☑ Do you have a recognition system linked to values?

☑ Do you hold regular 1:1 feedback conversation?

☑ Do your team members appreciate each other — not just you appreciating them?

☑ Does your calendar include time to reflect on culture?

If not — start with just **one ritual this week**.

And add others gradually.

Daily Leadership Habits for Founders:

You can hire the best people.

You can build the strongest systems.

You can define values and create rituals.

But none of it will stick if *you*, the founder, don't walk the talk.

"Your daily habits are louder than your team handbook."

In every MSME, culture flows from the top.

The team doesn't just watch what you say — they watch how you behave.

They notice:

- How you speak during pressure
- How you respond to failure
- How you treat customers and vendors
- How you handle feedback
- How consistent you are with your values

In this section, we'll explore the **daily habits that shape culture from the top down** and how to incorporate them into your leadership rhythm.

Because the fastest way to change your culture is to change your **example.**

The Problem: Founder Inconsistency Confuses Culture

In many MSMEs, the founder is unknowingly the biggest culture bottleneck.

Here's what often happens:

- They preach "client-first" but delay in responding to complaints
- They promote "teamwork" but favour certain employees
- They talk about "learning" but get angry at mistakes

- They want initiative — but override decisions too quickly

This inconsistency sends mixed signals.

The result?

- Good team members become quiet
- Average performers mimic the wrong behaviours
- Everyone starts playing it safe

Over time, a silent message spread:

"Just follow instructions. Don't think too much."

That's how innovation dies.

That's how ownership disappears.

The Agitation: Without Conscious Habits, Old Patterns Take Over

Most founders are not *trying* to be inconsistent.

They're just busy. Distracted. Stressed.

So they revert to whatever feels urgent at the moment.

And in that moment:

- Values are forgotten
- Emotions take over
- Leadership becomes reactive

But your team is still watching.

And they're forming conclusions like:

- "Boss doesn't mean what he says"
- "Nobody cares about values — only results."
- "Play it safe, don't take risks."

This is how culture *decays silently* — even with all the right tools.

The Solution: Leadership by Habit, Not Just Intention

Strong leadership is not about grand gestures.

It's about **small, repeatable habits** that show your team what truly matters.

Let's look at five high-impact daily/weekly habits that build trust, model values, and set the cultural tone.

Habit 1: Start Your Day with Cultural Alignment

Before diving into calls, emails, or team issues, take 10 minutes every morning to:

☑ Review your top 3 priorities

☑ Revisit your team's values

☑ Ask: *"How can I live one value visibly today?"*

Example:

If the value is "Own the Outcome," you might decide to personally follow up on a delayed client delivery — not to micromanage, but to show responsibility.

This builds internal alignment—and external consistency.

Habit 2: Publicly Praise One Team Member Daily

Every day, take 2 minutes to:

- Notice one act of ownership, effort, or alignment
- Call it out in your team group, stand-up, or in-person

Say:

"Today, I appreciate Manish for taking full responsibility for onboarding new clients. He lived our value of 'Speed with Accuracy.' Well done."

This habit reinforces:

- The behaviours you want more of
- The values you want to anchor
- The belief that *someone is noticing*

Over time, your praise shapes their performance.

Habit 3: Respond to Mistakes with Curiosity, Not Anger

When things go wrong, your **reaction becomes policy**.

If you shout, blame, or sarcastically criticise — the culture shifts towards fear.

Instead, use this 3-step script:

1. **Acknowledge** the issue
2. **Ask** what happened (without interrupting)
3. **Reflect together** on what can be changed in the system, not just the person

Say:

"Let's break down what happened. What was missed? How can we prevent it next time?"

This shows your team that learning is valued more than perfection. It creates a culture of **psychological safety**, which is critical for ownership.

Habit 4: Share One Insight or Learning Weekly

Great leaders teach.

Every week, take 5–10 minutes to share:

- A story from your own journey
- A lesson from a mistake
- A client insight
- A business principle
- A mindset shift

Example:

"I realised I was spending too much time on approvals last week. So I've started trusting the process more and delegating faster."

These moments make you human. And humans inspire humans.

Habit 5: Block "Thinking Time" on Your Calendar

You are the cultural architect, and architects need space to design.

Block at least 1 hour per week to:

- Reflect on team energy
- Identify patterns (good or bad)
- Think about your own leadership habits
- Plan the next steps in strengthening the culture

This is not a luxury. It's your **strategic responsibility.**

Because a founder who never reflects eventually becomes reactive.

Bonus: Use a Leadership Habits Tracker

Keep a simple checklist to track these habits weekly:

Day	Cultural Focus	Recognition Given?	Handled Mistake Calmly?	Shared Learning?
Monday	Own the Outcome	✓	✓	✗
Tuesday	Client First	✓	✓	✓

Even 70–80% consistency creates huge cultural momentum.

"Your team won't become what you say. They'll become what you show — every day."

Quick Self-Check: Are You Modelling the Culture You Want?

- ☑ Do you start your day with intentional leadership?

- ☑ Do you praise aligned behaviour regularly?

- ☑ Do you respond calmly when things go wrong?

- ☑ Do you teach and share your learnings?

- ☑ Do you create time to reflect and refine your leadership?

If not — don't wait for a better time.

Start today. Start small. Start visibly.

Accountability Without Micromanagement:

You've created systems.

You've defined values.

You've started modelling the behaviour you want to see.

But now comes a crucial test:

How do you **ensure performance** — without breathing down people's necks?

How do you track what's getting done — without becoming the bottleneck?

How do you maintain high standards — without creating fear or frustration?

> **"Micromanagement kills initiative. Lack of accountability kills performance."**

What you need is a balance.

This section is about building that balance through **smart, respectful, and rhythmic accountability systems** that keep your team aligned, responsible, and high-performing — *without needing your constant push.*

Let's build a culture of **commitment over control**.

The Problem: Accountability Is Missing — Or Misused

Most MSME teams operate in one of two extremes:

⬤ Scenario 1: No Accountability

- Tasks are assigned verbally or casually
- Deadlines are fuzzy
- Follow-ups are inconsistent
- Team members forget or delay
- Founder gets frustrated and starts doing it themselves

Result:

People feel no pressure, and results stay average.

⬤ Scenario 2: Over-Accountability (Micromanagement)

- The founder checks on everything every hour
- The team is scared to make mistakes
- No one experiments
- Work happens, but morale is low

Result:

The team feels suffocated. Founder feels burdened. Growth slows down.

Neither extreme works.

What you need is **a clear, consistent, non-emotional** performance system—one that respects your team and protects your time.

The Agitation: Without Systems, Pressure Becomes Personal

When accountability is not systemised, it becomes emotional.

People start saying:

- "Boss is angry again."
- "He's always after me."
- "It depends on his mood."
- "I can't say anything — he'll snap."

You may think you're being firm.

But your team experiences it as **random pressure**.

Over time, this creates:

- Avoidance
- Excuses
- Low initiative
- High attrition

That's not accountability. That's **emotional control.**

Let's fix it with **structure and clarity.**

Step 1: Set Clear Expectations (Outcome > Activity)

Don't just assign tasks. Assign **outcomes.**

Here's the difference:

- ✗ "Please call the leads"
- ☑ "Convert 10 out of 50 leads this week. Update CRM daily."
- ✗ "Manage the dispatches"
- ☑ "Ensure 95% on-time dispatch this week. Escalate issues within 12 hours."

Every task should have the following:

☑ A clear owner

☑ A deadline

☑ A success metric

☑ A communication channel

This clarity alone will solve 60% of your performance issues.

Step 2: Use Weekly Scorecards (Not Memory or Mood)

Create a **simple Weekly Scorecard** for each department or team member.

Example:

Name	Role	Key Metric	Target	Actual	Status	Comments
Ramesh	Sales Lead	Weekly Conversions	10	8	◯	2 follow-ups pending
Asha	Ops Manager	On-Time Dispatch %	95%	97%	☑	Excellent recovery
Preeti	Accounts	Weekly Collection (₹)	₹2,00,000	₹1,85,000	◯	One client delayed

Use colours:

- ☑ Green = On track
- ◯ Yellow = Slight deviation
- ⬤ Red = Immediate attention

Share this every **Monday morning**.

Let the **team update it themselves** — that's how ownership grows.

Step 3: Run Weekly Accountability Reviews (30–45 mins)

Once a week, sit with your team or leads and review:

- What was promised vs. what was done
- Why something slipped (if it did)
- What's the new commitment for this week
- Any support or decisions required from you

Keep the tone factual, not emotional. No blaming. No shaming. Just alignment. This rhythm builds **reliability** — across departments.

Step 4: Use Monthly 1:1s for Deep Accountability

Scorecards show numbers.

But monthly **1:1 check-in** reveal:

- What's blocking progress
- What's causing stress
- Where team members need support
- What does their next level of growth look like

Structure the 1:1 like this:

1. Review Scorecard
2. Ask: "What went well this month?"
3. Ask: "What's one area we can improve together?"
4. Discuss growth goals (training, role clarity, etc.)
5. Ask: "How can I lead you better?"

This builds **trust and performance** together.

Step 5: Address Slips with Calm, Not Conflict

When someone misses a target — don't jump to judgment.

Use the **"Explain, Explore, Escalate"** method:

1. Explain

Let them share what happened — without interruption.

2. Explore

Ask:

- "What could have been done differently?"
- "Where did the process fail?"
- "How can we prevent it next time?"

3. Escalate (if repeated)

If the same mistake repeats thrice — escalate to a formal warning, training, or role change.

This creates fairness — not fear.

Quick Self-Check: Do You Have Respectful Accountability?

☑ Are expectations outcome-based, not vague?

☑ Is performance tracked weekly with scorecards?

☑ Do team members self-report, not wait to be chased?

☑ Are reviews regular, not emotional?

☑ Is feedback honest — but growth-focused?

If not — start building this rhythm now.

Because consistency beats intensity every time.

Final Thought

Great culture is not soft.

It's strong, clear, and respectful.

It supports your team with trust.

It challenges them with structure.

And it frees you, the founder, to grow the business — not chase tasks.

You've now built the foundation of a high-ownership team culture.

Next, we'll explore how to **retain your best performers** and **build repeatable customer loyalty** — so that your team and clients stay with you for the long haul.

Let's create the engine of **retention and repeat growth.**

Chapter 8: Build a Business That Grows from the Inside

Most MSMEs spend a lot of time, energy, and money chasing *new* customers.

New leads, New ads, New calls, New discounts.

But what if the secret to smart, sustainable, and stress-free growth was not in the *next* client...

...but in the **last one**?

"Retention is not just a strategy — it's your most powerful growth engine."

While everyone else fights over new traffic, smart MSMEs quietly scale by retaining their customers, nurturing relationships, and creating repeat revenue — without extra marketing costs.

This chapter will help you shift from a "one-time sale" mindset to a **"lifetime value" mindset**.

We'll show you how to build loyalty, repeat purchases, and customer-driven referrals using simple, actionable systems that any small business can implement.

The Problem: MSMEs Are Addicted to Acquisition

Let's look at how most MSMEs grow:

- The new lead comes in
- Quote is sent
- Deal is closed
- Delivery is made
- That's it — the customer is forgotten

No follow-up, No feedback, No nurturing, No reactivation.

So, the business must work twice as hard every month to stay at the same level.

And when new leads dry up, or ad costs rise — the panic begins.

This is not a marketing issue.

It's a **model issue.**

You're building a leaky bucket — instead of creating a fountain.

The Agitation: Lack of Retention Creates Exhaustion

Here's what happens when you don't focus on repeat and retention:

- You burn money on ads to replace old customers
- Sales become unpredictable and seasonal
- You lose customer trust after one transaction
- Your team is always in closing mode, never in relationship mode
- You never get to enjoy the **compounding effect** of long-term clients

The result?

- Higher cost per sale
- Lower profit margins
- Constant stress to "bring in new business."

But retention flips this.

When one happy customer keeps buying, referring, and trusting — your revenue multiplies without your effort multiplying.

The Solution: Build a Retention & Repeat Engine

This chapter walks you through **five key components** of creating a business that doesn't just attract — but retains and re-engages customers consistently.

Each section gives you practical tools to apply immediately, even starting from scratch.

Let's look at what's coming up.

Deliver Delight: Go Beyond Product to Create Emotional Wins

Customers don't stay because you're cheap.

They stay because you make them feel:

- Valued
- Heard
- Respected
- Understood

In this section, you'll learn:

- How to create a "Wow Experience" at key customer touchpoints
- How to set up simple delight rituals that create emotional stickiness
- How small gestures lead to massive loyalty

Because in business, people don't remember the invoice — they remember how they felt.

Build a Repeat Sales Path – Make the Second Sale Easy

Most MSMEs focus only on getting the first sale.

But the second sale is where the *real profit* lies — because it costs nothing to acquire.

This section helps you:

- Map your products/services into repeatable offers
- Design upsells, cross-sells, and reactivation strategies
- Use tools like WhatsApp campaigns, reorder reminders, and loyalty offers

So that one customer becomes five transactions — not just one.

Start a Customer Relationship System: Stay Top of Mind

In today's noisy market, if you're not visible — you're forgettable.

This section shows you how to create:

- Monthly newsletters or WhatsApp updates
- Birthday/anniversary follow-ups
- Educational drip campaigns
- Personalised check-ins

You'll use simple tools (like TeleCRM, WA Sender, and New Zenler) to build **customer intimacy at scale**.

Because strong relationships reduce price resistance and increase referral readiness.

Turn Clients into Promoters – Referral Systems That Work

Happy clients love to refer. But they often don't — unless you ask *strategically*.

In this section, you'll build a simple referral engine that includes:

- When to ask
- What to offer
- How to reward
- How to track
- How to make referrals *feel* natural, not forced

You'll learn how to make every client feel like a **brand ambassador**, not just a buyer.

Track LTV (Lifetime Value) – Grow the Client, Not Just the Sale

The businesses that survive are not the ones with the most sales but the **longest-lasting customers**.

In this final section, you'll learn how to:

- Calculate LTV for your business
- Segment clients by value and loyalty
- Identify your top 20% — and invest in them
- Use a simple Client Tracker to plan long-term upsells and offers

Once you start thinking in LTV, everything changes — from how you market to how you serve.

What You'll Gain from This Chapter

☑ A low-cost strategy to grow without chasing leads

☑ Systems to create delight, stay connected, and re-sell

☑ Referral tools to multiply your best clients

☑ Insight into your most valuable customer segments

☑ A shift from effort-based growth to trust-based growth

Time to Build Your Growth Engine from the Inside

The best businesses don't need to shout.

They build loyalty so deep that their customers do the marketing for them.

Retention is not a bonus.

It's a **strategy for survival, scale, and peace of mind.**

Deliver Delight:

Why do some customers never return...

...while others come back again and again — bringing their friends along.

It's rarely about price.

It's not just about quality.

It's rarely about features.

It's about **how the customer feels.**

"Product satisfaction gets you a transaction. Emotional delight gets you a loyal customer."

In this section, we'll help you build one of the most powerful business assets an MSME can have—a system for creating *delight*.

Not random surprises. Not expensive gifts.

But *repeatable, consistent emotional wins* that make your customers feel so valued that they **never want to leave.**

The Problem: Most MSMEs Stop at Delivery

Let's look at the typical MSME customer journey:

- Customer enquires
- Price is shared
- Order is placed
- Product/service is delivered

- Payment is received

Done.

Then what?

Usually... nothing.

No follow-up, No thank you, No check-in, No surprise, No emotional connection.

The transaction ends, and so does the relationship.

And yet the founder wonders: *"Why don't people come back?"*

The answer is simple: **You gave a product. They wanted an experience.**

The Agitation: Satisfied Customers Leave. Delighted Customers Stay.

Here's the silent trap:

A satisfied customer has **no complaints**.

But also, there is no **reason** to stay loyal.

They may:

- Try a cheaper competitor
- Forget you exist
- Be swayed by the next ad they see
- Feel unappreciated or unseen

And in crowded markets, **being forgettable is fatal.**

Only when you create delight do you build **emotional hooks** that make people return, recommend you, and forgive small hiccups.

Delight is what separates **vendors** from **brands**.

Let's learn how to do it without big budgets or complex systems.

Step 1: Identify the Emotional Moments in Your Customer Journey

Delight doesn't happen at every step.

It happens at **key moments**.

Your job is to identify and enhance these "Emotional Windows."

Examples:

Stage	Emotional Opportunity
First Enquiry	Make the response warm and personalised
Order Confirmation	Reassure, excite, and thank them
Delivery/Completion	Surprise them with a small value-add
After-Sale Follow-Up	Check-in genuinely, not just for payment
Repeat Purchase	Recognise loyalty and say, "Welcome back."

Start mapping this for your business:

"Where can we create a smile?"

Step 2: Create Small, Repeatable Delight Rituals

Delight doesn't mean expensive gifts.

It means **thoughtfulness**.

Let's look at some practical, low-cost examples you can systemise:

- 🎁 *Handwritten thank-you note with first order*
- 🏷️ *Branded sticker/seal that says "Packed with care just for you."*
- 📞 *3-day post-delivery feedback call asking, "How was the experience?"*
- 📝 *Free checklist or tip sheet with the product*
- 📱 *Personalised WhatsApp messages on their birthday*
- 🤝 *Calling repeat buyers by name and acknowledging their loyalty*

These actions cost ₹10–₹100. But they deliver **₹10,000 worth of goodwill**.

Create a **Delight SOP** — a checklist your team follows for every client.

Step 3: Use the "First-Time Wow" Principle

The first impression sets the tone for loyalty.

Create a dedicated **First-Time Customer Flow**:

- Welcome call/message from the founder or senior team
- First-use guidance video or demo
- A thank-you email/story that introduces your journey
- Small gift or surprise on first delivery
- Customer photo/testimonial wall: "Our newest family member"

This turns a transaction into a **relationship start** — not just a file in your system.

Step 4: Empower Your Team to Delight on the Spot

Your systems are great. But your people are better.

Train your frontline team (sales, delivery, service) to look for **opportunities to delight**.

Give them the freedom to:

- Offer a free add-on when a customer is unhappy
- Send a surprise "We Miss You" message
- Escalate small issues before the client has to complain
- Send a personal voice note to say thank you

Empower them with a **"Delight Budget"** — even ₹500/month — to take the initiative without needing permission.

It's not an expense. It's an **investment in loyalty**.

Step 5: Capture & Celebrate Customer Delight Stories

Delight moments aren't just good for the customer — they're marketing gold.

Create a ritual of capturing:

- Customer thank-you notes
- Testimonials
- Repeat client screenshots
- Video feedback
- Before-after transformation stories

Use these in:

- Social media content
- WhatsApp updates
- Team huddles ("Delight Story of the Week")
- Onboarding kits for new clients

When your team sees the joy they create — they're more likely to do it again.

Bonus: Build a "Delight Tracker"

Create a simple Google Sheet with columns:

Customer Name	Date	Type of Delight	Response	Team Member
Meena Traders	3 May	Birthday call	Smiled, shared feedback	Preeti

Track weekly. Review monthly.

Watch how trust deepens — one small gesture at a time.

Quick Self-Check: Are You Delighting — or Just Delivering?

☑ Do you have a clear process for first-time customer experience?

☑ Do you surprise customers with anything *after* payment is done?

☑ Does your team know they can delight — not just deliver?

☑ Are you capturing delightful stories and celebrating them internally?

If not — start with **one simple delight moment** this week.

It will come back to you tenfold.

Build a Repeat Sales Path:

Getting a new customer is exciting.

But turning that customer into a **repeat buyer** — that's where the real profit begins.

Unfortunately, most MSMEs stop after the first transaction.

They say:

- "Once they need it again, they'll come."
- "If they're happy, they'll remember us."
- "We don't want to sound pushy."

But in today's crowded market, being silent is the same as being invisible.

"A repeat sale is not luck — it's the result of a system."

This section is about building that system.

A simple, non-salesy repeat sales path that turns one-time buyers into long-term revenue — without needing new ad spends every time.

The Problem: No Path = No Repeat

Here's what happens in most MSMEs:

- The sale is made
- Product/service is delivered
- The customer is left alone
- The team moves on to the next lead

- The database gathers dust

You're spending 10X effort to keep filling the top of the funnel...

...while ignoring the **gold mine** you've already built.

This leads to:

- Unpredictable revenue
- Pressure on marketing and sales
- Loss of customer attention over time

In simple words — you're leaking money.

The Agitation: Even Happy Customers Forget

Many founders assume that happy customers will automatically return.

But here's the reality:

Even satisfied clients **forget you exist** if:

- You don't stay in touch
- You don't remind them of your offerings
- You don't make it easy to buy again
- You don't introduce them to new services/products

They don't hate you. They're just distracted.

Your job is to **make the next sale feel natural** — not forced.

And that requires structure.

The Solution: Map Your Repeat Sales Path

Let's break this down into five steps to build a smart, repeat-friendly system:

Step 1: Identify What Can Be Repeated

Not all products/services have a natural repeat cycle.

But *almost every business* can create one.

Ask:

- Is your product consumable or renewable?
- Can it be upgraded, extended, or re-purchased?
- Can you bundle related products or add-ons?
- Can you offer seasonal or occasion-based packages?
- Can you launch a new line for past clients?

Examples:

Business Type	Repeat Opportunity
Bakery	Monthly celebration boxes, subscription kits
Coaching Institute	Advanced courses, alum programs
Garment Manufacturer	Festive collection for old buyers
Interior Designer	Annual maintenance, decor upgrades
Industrial Supplier	Bulk reordering, AMC packages

Look at your own past clients and ask:

"What's the next thing they need?"

Step 2: Create a "Next Step" Offer Path

Once you know what to offer, **design the flow**.

Think of it like this:

1. First product → Intro experience
2. Second offer → Complimentary upgrade or refill
3. Third offer → Premium bundle or extended service
4. Fourth offer → Subscription, retainer, or loyalty offer

This gives your business a **built-in revenue staircase.**

It also helps your sales team know exactly what to promote — without waiting for a lead to ask.

Use a visual tool like a funnel chart or staircase graphic to teach this to your team.

Step 3: Build Timing-Based Follow-Up Triggers

Even if your product is great, **timing matters.**

You need to reach the customer **before** they forget you and **when** they will most likely need you again.

Create follow-up triggers like:

- ⏱ 3 days after delivery → Ask for feedback
- ⏱ 10 days later → Share a care tip or free guide
- ⏱ 30 days later → Recommend a refill or related product
- ⏱ 60 days later → Offer loyalty coupon or bundle
- ⏱ 90 days later → Reconnect with a "We miss you" message

Use tools like:

- **WA Sender** for scheduled WhatsApp follow-ups
- **TeleCRM** for lead lifecycle management
- **Google Sheets + calendar reminders** for low-tech systems

Create a standard **Repeat Follow-Up Calendar** for your team.

Step 4: Use Personalised Communication

"Sir, Do you need something more?" is not a repeat sales strategy.

Instead, use **personalised, context-rich messaging** like:

- "Hi Rohit, since you ordered the Premium Toolkit last month, we've launched a new accessory that fits perfectly with it. Would you like a quick look?"
- "Meena Ji, many repeat clients love our 3-month home fragrance combo. Would you like a preview?"
- "Just for our returning customers — 10% off till this Sunday on your favourite flavour!"

This feels **helpful, not pushy**.

It makes the customer feel seen.

Step 5: Train Your Team to Spot Repeat Triggers

Your sales or service team must be trained to:

- ☑ Tag repeat buyers in the CRM

- ☑ Set reminders for second contact

- ☑ Offer relevant add-ons at the time of delivery

- ☑ Report "customer need signals" to your marketing team

Introduce a **Repeat Sales Tracker** where team members log:

Customer	Last Product	Repeat Opportunity	Action Taken	Result
Shah & Co.	Digital Signage	Annual Maintenance	Called on 1 Aug	In progress

Even one well-timed follow-up can lead to ₹10K+ repeat sales.

"The easiest customer to sell to is the one you've already earned."

Quick Self-Check: Are You Repeat-Ready?

✓ Do you have products/services that can be re-sold, refilled, or extended?

✓ Do you follow up post-sale with structured timing?

✓ Do you have a second offer mapped for each customer type?

✓ Is your team trained to suggest upgrades or cross-sells?

✓ Do you have a tool to track repeat sales performance?

If not — you're leaving money on the table *every single day*.

Start a Customer Relationship System:

Have you ever had a customer say:

"Oh! I forgot about you... we just bought this from someone else."

It stings. Not because they didn't like you but because they **forgot you existed.**

In the busyness of running an MSME, it's easy to focus on getting new customers and closing current orders. But what happens in between — when customers are *not* buying — is just as important.

"If you're not visible, you're forgettable. And forgotten businesses don't grow."

This section is about building a **Customer Relationship System** that keeps your brand in your clients' minds, hearts, and WhatsApp inboxes — *without being annoying, pushy, or salesy.*

Let's build a system that keeps your name at the forefront of your mind so that when they're ready to buy again or refer someone, they think of *you first.*

The Problem: Relationships Fade Without Contact

Here's the reality of most MSMEs:

- You speak to the customer during the sales process.
- You follow up to confirm the delivery or close payment.

- And after that... silence.

The customer hears nothing from you until you need something — or until they need something *and reach out* (if you're lucky).

This creates a "cold gap."

During that gap:

- The relationship weakens
- Competitors can sneak in
- Trust erodes due to inactivity
- Repeat or referral potential dies quietly
-

The Agitation: You Can't Rely on Memory or Mood

Many MSME founders think:

- "We'll call when we have something new."
- "They know where to find us."
- "I don't want to disturb them."
- "I'm too busy to keep following up."

But customers are bombarded with **ads, options, and distractions** every single day.

You'll disappear even from the happiest clients if you don't have a structured way to maintain a connection.

You need a system that works quietly in the background — **without you remembering anything manually.**

The Solution: A Simple, Personalised, Repeatable Customer Relationship System

This is not about fancy software or hiring a relationship manager.

This is about installing **low-cost, high-trust habits** into your business using basic tools.

Let's build it step by step.

Step 1: Create a Customer Touchpoint Calendar

You need a **12-month plan** that defines:

- *When* you reach out
- *How* you'll do it (WhatsApp, email, call, message)
- *What* you'll say (value-driven, not just "Buy now!")

Example Touchpoint Calendar:

Month	Activity	Tool Used
January	New Year wishes + loyalty coupon	WhatsApp Broadcast
February	Share free tips PDF (industry trends)	Email / WA PDF
March	Birthday follow-up for key clients	CRM + Reminder
April	Feedback form on last purchase	Google Form
May	"Miss You" message for inactive clients	TeleCRM + Call
June	New product sneak peek	WhatsApp Story
July	Share a client success story	Email Newsletter

You can repeat this cycle annually — or customise it for B2B/B2C needs.

This keeps you **relevant, helpful and remembered.**

Step 2: Use Tools That Work for You

You don't need an expensive CRM. Start with tools you or your team can already handle:

Purpose	Tool
Broadcasts	WA Sender, WhatsApp Business
Personalised Email	Mailchimp, Gmail templates
Birthday/Anniversary Reminders	Google Calendar, TeleCRM
Quick Visual Updates	Canva + WhatsApp Status
Collecting Feedback	Google Forms
Database Management	Google Sheets, Notion

Start with two tools. Master them. Then add more.

Remember: **Adoption > Ambition.**

Step 3: Segment Your Customers for Personal Relevance

Not all customers need the same updates.

Segment into:

- 🔘 High-value customers → monthly updates

- ◯ Regular clients → bi-monthly
- ⬤ Inactive clients → reactivation campaigns

Tag them in your CRM, spreadsheet, or WhatsApp list.

Send messages that make sense **for them** — not generic mass updates.

Example:

- "Hey Kiran, since you've bought from us three times this year, here's an exclusive early-bird offer on our new range."
- "Hi, Mr. Jain, we've missed you! Here's a quick 3-question feedback form. We'd love to reconnect."

Step 4: Use Stories, Not Just Sales

Customers remember stories — not specs.

Include:

- Customer transformation stories
- Behind the scenes of your team or process
- Founder thoughts or learnings
- Client testimonials with photos/videos
- Educational content (tips, trends, mistakes to avoid)

This builds **trust and connection**, even when they're not ready to buy.

You become **part of their mental ecosystem** — not just a vendor.

Step 5: Make It a Team Ritual

Relationship building is not just your job.

It's your team's rhythm.

Assign:

- One person to manage monthly client updates
- One day per month for team calls to top clients
- One WhatsApp story per week from your social media coordinator
- One testimonial to collect and share each Friday

This creates **consistency without chaos**.

Even 2–3 hours per month of structured effort can build lifetime loyalty.

"Customers leave when they don't feel remembered. Stay in touch — and you'll stay in business."

Quick Self-Check: Do You Have a Relationship System?

☑ Are you reaching out to customers even when they're not buying?

☑ Do you use tools to schedule or automate touchpoints?

☑ Are you telling stories and sharing value — not just offers?

☑ Is your team involved in building relationships?

☑ Do you have a calendar or rhythm that guides this process?

If not, you're losing visibility — visibility is the bridge to repeat sales.

Turn Clients into Promoters:

What if your next 10 best clients were brought to you…

…not by ads, cold calls, or exhibitions — but by your *existing* customers?

Think about it:

Your current clients already know your product.

They've already experienced your service.

They trust you.

Now imagine if they could be **trained and encouraged** to spread the word — naturally, willingly, and enthusiastically.

"Referrals aren't a bonus. They're a system you build."

This section will help you turn loyal customers into **active promoters** by creating a **referral system** that works quietly, consistently, and respectfully in the background.

No awkward begging.

No over-the-top incentives.

Just smart prompts and structured follow-through.

The Problem: Most Referrals Are Passive, Not Predictable

Many MSMEs believe referrals are *earned*, not *engineered*.

So they wait...

- Wait for the client to remember them
- Wait for the client to come across someone
- Wait for the perfect moment to happen

And when a referral does come, it feels like luck — not leverage.

However, the real problem is this: **most MSMEs never ask.**

Or if they do, they ask like this:

"If you know anyone, do let us know."

Vague. Passive. Easily forgotten.

That's not a referral system. That's wishful thinking.

The Agitation: You're Ignoring Your Most Powerful Sales Channel

Without a structured referral system:

- You keep spending money to acquire new leads
- You miss the chance to turn one sale into three

- You stay unknown in circles where your client already has influence
- You lose trust-based opportunities to competitors

And worst of all — you stop compounding your reputation.

Meanwhile, your happy customers *want* to refer you.

But they either forget, don't know how, or feel awkward about it.

You need to make it **easy, exciting, and expected.**

The Solution: Build a Simple, Systematic Referral Engine

Let's create a five-step system that doesn't just *hope* for referrals — it *creates* them.

You don't need a fancy affiliate platform.

Just tools you already have — and the right communication.

Step 1: Ask at the Right Time

Timing matters.

The best moment to ask for a referral is when the **customer is happiest.**

That could be:

- Right after a successful delivery

- When they give positive feedback
- When they reorder
- When they share appreciation on WhatsApp
- During your follow-up call or visit

Train your team to listen for signals like:

"This was really smooth!"

"I loved your packaging!"

"Service was quicker than expected!"

That's your cue to ask. Not beg — nudge.

Step 2: Use a Simple Referral Script

Don't say, *"Please refer us to your friends."*

Instead, use something like:

"We loved working with you and are so glad you're happy. We mostly grow through referrals — would you be open to introducing us to someone who might benefit too?"

Or:

"Many of our best clients come through good people like you. I'd be grateful for a connection if anyone comes to mind."

Keep it warm. Keep it human. Keep it honest.

And always **personalise.**

Step 3: Make It Easy for Them to Refer

Referrals die when the process is hard.

Make it effortless by giving them:

- A short WhatsApp message they can forward
- A pre-written intro email or SMS
- A QR code or referral link to share
- A physical card they can pass to someone
- A "Refer & Reward" flyer with clear steps

Example:

"Hey! I'm just forwarding you a contact. They did a great job for us—high quality and on time. Reach out if you need something similar."

Even better: Offer to **draft the message for them** and let them edit it.

Step 4: Add a Small Incentive or Thank-You

People don't refer to rewards. They refer you because they trust you.

But a small thank-you goes a long way.

You can offer:

- A ₹250 gift voucher
- A small discount on the next order
- A free upgrade or surprise gift

- A "Referral Champion" shoutout on social media
- A handwritten note or voice message from the founder

If they refer multiple clients, send something unexpected.

They'll never forget it.

And they'll likely refer again.

Step 5: Track Referrals & Celebrate Them

Referrals that aren't tracked die in silence.

Use a simple **Referral Tracker** in Google Sheets or your CRM:

Referrer Name	Client Referred	Status	Reward Sent	Notes
Meena Traders	Agrawal Exports	Onboarded	Sent voucher	2nd referral
Ravi Kumar	Patel & Sons	In process	–	Call this week

Every month, review:

- Who referred
- Who needs to be thanked
- Who deserves a surprise bonus

Celebrate your promoters in team meetings.

This motivates both the team and clients.

"Referrals don't need to be lucky. They need to be intentional."

Bonus: Create a "Client Circle" Program

Invite your best referrers into an exclusive club:

- Early access to new products
- Monthly learning newsletter
- Birthday/anniversary surprises
- First invite to events or webinars

Call it:

- "Insider Circle"
- "Loyal Leader Club"
- "Growth Partner Program"

This gives them a **sense of belonging** — and makes them *want* to bring others into the family.

Quick Self-Check: Are You Referral-Ready?

☑ Do you ask for referrals at the right moment?

☑ Is your team trained with a script or prompt?

☑ Do you provide shareable messages or links?

☑ Are referrers thanked — every time?

☑ Do you track and review referrals regularly?

If not, you're leaving your most powerful marketing on mute.

Turn it on — and let your clients become your growth team.

Track LTV (Lifetime Value):

Imagine this:

You have two customers.

- Customer A places one large order worth ₹50,000.
- Customer B places smaller, regular orders of ₹15,000 every quarter for 3 years.

At first glance, Customer A seems more valuable.

But over time...

Customer B brings in ₹1,80,000 — *and more trust, feedback, and referrals.*

This is the difference between **transactional thinking** and **relationship thinking**.

"Real business growth doesn't come from more sales. It comes from deeper value with the right customers."

This section will help you understand, measure, and grow **Customer Lifetime Value (LTV)** — the total revenue a client generates during their relationship with your business.

When you track LTV, you stop chasing everyone and focus on those who grow your business.

The Problem: MSMEs Focus on Today's Sale, Not the Long-Term Value

Most founders only look at:

- Monthly sales
- Pre-order value
- Daily targets
- Who paid fastest

But they rarely ask:

- Who's stayed with us the longest?
- Who refers us the most?
- Who comes back again and again?
- Who upgrades over time?

So they end up:

- Rewarding noisy customers, not loyal ones
- Ignoring their top 20%
- Giving equal effort to low-value clients
- Designing offers without segmentation

And the result?

There is no clarity on where to double down.

The Agitation: Not Tracking LTV = Wasted Focus

When you don't track LTV:

- You treat every customer the same
- You can't identify your best segments
- You end up over-serving the least profitable clients
- You under-serve the ones with real potential
- You miss upsell, cross-sell, and retention opportunities

Over time, your marketing becomes broad.

Your team gets tired.

And your growth plateaus — because effort is not matched to return.

You don't need more clients.

You need more value from the **right** clients.

The Solution: Understand, Calculate, and Grow LTV

Let's break this down into a simple 5-step approach you can implement — even if you're not using fancy software.

Step 1: Define What LTV Means for Your Business

LTV is the total revenue (or profit) a customer brings during their journey with you.

LTV = Average Order Value × Number of Transactions per Year × Retention Period (in years)

Example:

- Average order = ₹15,000
- Buys 4 times a year
- Retains for 2 years
- → LTV = ₹15,000 × 4 × 2 = ₹1,20,000

You can also include referral value (if known), upgrade potential and upsell history

The more accurate your estimate, the better your focus.

Step 2: Segment Your Customers by LTV

Not all customers are equal.

Use a simple sheet or CRM to divide clients into three categories:

Segment	Criteria	Focus Strategy
Tier A – High LTV	Repeat purchases, upgrades, referrals	Retain, reward, upsell
Tier B – Medium LTV	Occasional buyers	Nurture, educate, reactivate
Tier C – Low LTV	One-time or price-sensitive	Minimal effort, auto-serve

This helps you **prioritise your team's energy.**

Your top 20% often generates 60–80% of your profit.

Step 3: Create LTV Boosting Opportunities

Once you know who's valuable — help them go further.

Ways to increase LTV:

- 💡 Introduce add-ons, upgrades, or bundles
- 💡 Offer longer-term retainers or subscriptions
- 💡 Launch loyalty programs for repeat clients
- 💡 Invite them into beta tests or VIP groups
- 💡 Give them first access to new launches
- 💡 Create annual "thank you" surprise boxes

You're not pushing sales — you're **serving deeper.**

Step 4: Track and Review LTV Regularly

Once a quarter, review:

☑ Who are our top 10 highest LTV clients?

☑ What patterns do they share (industry, geography, product type)?

☑ Who dropped off — and why?

☑ Which new clients look promising?

Use a basic **LTV Tracker** like this:

Client Name	Total Orders	Avg. Value	Retention Period	LTV	Tier
Meena Textiles	8	₹22,000	2.5 years	₹4,40,000	A
Surya Exports	3	₹9,000	1 year	₹27,000	C

This becomes your **strategy dashboard** for repeat growth.

Step 5: Align Team, Offers & Support with LTV Segments

Your entire business must reflect this focus.

- Your **sales team** should follow up faster with Tier A leads
- Your **support team** should resolve Tier A issues urgently
- Your **founder time** should go to top-tier clients
- Your **offers and marketing** should be shaped by Tier A feedback

Even small tweaks in prioritising can 2X your profit — *without increasing your workload.*

"You don't need more clients. You need deeper value from the right ones."

Bonus: Use LTV to Guide Client Exit Too

If a customer:

- Always delays payments
- Is it rude or toxic
- Negotiates every time
- Never refers to or repeats

...it's okay to **let them go.**

Free your energy for those who match your values and value your work.

That's not arrogance. It's **strategic maturity.**

Quick Self-Check: Are You LTV-Driven?

- ☑ Do you know your top 10 clients by lifetime value?

- ☑ Do you track repeat purchases and referrals?

- ☑ Do you segment and prioritise based on value?

- ☑ Are you offering deeper value — not just more discounts?

- ☑ Does your team know who your best clients are?

If not — start this quarter.

It will change the way you plan, serve, and grow.

Chapter 9: Scale Without Chaos

Build Systems That Run Without You

You've worked hard to bring your business to this stage.

You've cracked sales.

You've built a loyal customer base.

You've structured your team.

You've even created repeat revenue engines.

But now comes a *new* challenge — and a dangerous one:

How do you grow without breaking what you've built?

Because here's what most MSMEs experience when they try to scale:

- More orders = more confusion
- Bigger teams = more dependency
- Higher targets = lower margins
- Faster growth = more mistakes

- Founder's stress = skyrockets

Growth becomes chaotic, stressful, and overwhelming.

"If your business needs you more as it grows, you're not scaling. You're just stretching."

In this chapter, we'll show you how to build a **scalable business foundation** that doesn't fall apart when you grow and doesn't trap you when things get busy.

You'll learn how to install five core systems that allow your business to expand without friction — and with your *peace of mind intact.*

The Problem: Scaling Increases Volume — and Pressure

In the early stages, you can survive with jugaad.

A few handwritten notes.

Some verbal updates.

There are a few team calls here and there.

Memory-based approvals.

Gut-feel decisions.

But when you try to grow:

- Orders multiply
- Clients diversify

- Team expands
- Timelines shrink
- Expectations rise

Suddenly, what worked before starts **breaking silently.**

You spend your day firefighting instead of strategising.

Your best team members feel lost or overworked.

Your service quality drops.

And *you* become the bottleneck — again.

The Agitation: Growth Without Systems = Founder's Trap

Without proper systems, scaling becomes:

- Emotionally draining
- Operationally messy
- Financially risky

And instead of enjoying growth, you start:

- Dreading the next big order
- Delaying expansion decisions
- Micromanaging every issue
- Dreaming of "someday" hiring a COO
- Losing control over quality, timelines, and team accountability

This is where many MSMEs **stall** — not because they lack ambition, but because they lack **scalable systems.**

It's time to change that.

The Solution: Build a Self-Scaling Business Engine

This chapter will walk you through the **five foundational systems** every growth-ready MSME must install — regardless of size or industry.

Each system will help you **reduce chaos, increase consistency, and create clarity** — so that your business scales with strength, not stress.

Let's take a quick look at what's ahead.

9.1: SOPs that Work – Turn Chaos into Consistency

What happens when someone leaves?

What happens when someone new joins?

What happens when volume spikes?

If your answer is *"I'll figure it out"* — you're scaling on hope.

In this section, you'll learn how to:

- Build SOPs (Standard Operating Procedures) even if you hate documentation
- Use templates, checklists, and simple videos
- Make SOPs usable for frontline staff
- Create a "knowledge base" that grows with your business

You'll go from memory-based operations to **repeatable excellence.**

9.2: Smart Task Management – Know Who's Doing What, By When

"Who is handling this?"

"Has that task been completed?"

"Who did the last follow-up?"

If you hear these questions every day — your task system is broken.

This section helps you:

- Set up a clear task dashboard for you and your team
- Allocate, track, and close tasks without chasing
- Use tools like Trello, ClickUp, Google Sheets, or even WhatsApp in structured ways
- Install a "Task Review Rhythm" that keeps work moving without reminders

The result? **Less follow-up, more follow-through.**

9.3: Founder Dashboards – Take Control Without Micromanaging

You don't need 27 reports. You need **five indicators** that show the health of your business.

This section helps you build:

- A simple, visual Founder Dashboard
- Key metrics to track weekly (sales, ops, cash flow, team)
- Scorecard-style visibility without complexity
- A weekly review rhythm that keeps you in command

Instead of asking 10 questions every day, you'll glance at your dashboard and know **exactly where to focus.**

9.4: Time Systems for Scale – Free Up the Founder

As the business grows, so does the **demand on your time**.

You need a system to:

- Block deep work hours
- Limit daily distractions
- Set meeting rhythms
- Protect thinking time
- Delegate decisions

This section will help you design a **founder calendar** that serves the business *without consuming your life*.

Scaling with stress is not scaling; it's *suffering*.

9.5: Ownership Transfer – Step Back Without Slipping

You want to scale.

You want the team to lead.

But you also want quality, speed, and trust.

In this final section, we'll help you:

- Build a delegation framework that transfers not just tasks but also *ownership*
- Set decision boundaries for teams
- Create checkpoints, not micromanagement
- Spot future leaders inside your team
- Design an "Ownership Transfer Canvas" for any key process

This is how you **scale with peace.**

You'll step back without losing control.

What You'll Gain from This Chapter

☑ A structured way to handle growth

☑ Tools and checklists for repeatable execution

☑ Visibility into what's working and what's breaking

☑ Freedom from founder-dependency

☑ A business that runs smoothly — even when you're not in the room

Time to Scale Smart — Not Just Big

Growth is exciting.

But **smart scale** is what gives you freedom.

With the right systems, your business becomes a vehicle — not a prison.

Turn the page, and let's build your *scaling engine* that runs on structure, not struggle.

SOPs That Work:

Turn Chaos into Consistency

Imagine this:

Your top team member takes a sudden leave.

A new hire joins but doesn't know the process.

A customer complains about an error — but no one's sure *who* is responsible or *what* went wrong.

Now imagine the same situation...

But instead of confusion, there's clarity.

- The new team member opens a shared folder titled "Onboarding SOP."
- The delivery issue is traced back using a 3-step dispatch checklist.
- A junior executive confidently solves a repeat problem — without asking the founder.

That's the power of SOPs.

"If it's important — it should be written down."

SOPs (Standard Operating Procedures) are not fancy manuals meant for big companies.

They're **clarity tools** — designed to reduce stress, avoid repetition, and make your business more *independent of you*.

In this section, we'll explain how to create simple, usable, scalable SOPs that free up your time, reduce mistakes, and build a consistent customer experience *without needing to hire consultants or create binders of documents.*

The Problem: MSMEs Run on Memory, Not Methods

Let's be honest.

Most small businesses rely on:

- Verbal instructions
- WhatsApp messages
- "You've seen how it's done — do it that way."
- Excel sheets saved on one laptop
- Team knowledge stored in people's heads

This works when you're small and stable.

But the moment you:

- Hire new people
- Expand locations
- Take on bigger clients
- Step away from daily operations

...everything starts breaking.

You see:

- Missed follow-ups
- Delivery errors
- Team blaming each other

- Founder re-explaining the same things every week
- Customer dissatisfaction due to inconsistency

This is not a team problem.

It's a **systems gap.**

The Agitation: Every Mistake Costs You Growth

When there's no SOP:

- New hires take months to settle
- Old team members become gatekeepers
- Tasks depend on memory, not structure
- You end up saying: *"I have to look after everything."*

Every small mistake becomes a big delay.

Every delay becomes a dent in your brand.

And every dent reduces your trust in the team — and their trust in your leadership.

You start dreading holidays, new projects, and delegation.

But it doesn't have to be this way.

The Solution: Build SOPs That Are Simple, Used, and Useful

You don't need 50-page documents.

You need **working SOPs** — short, visual, and accessible.

Let's break the system into five easy steps.

Step 1: Identify the "Chaos Zones" in Your Business

Start by asking:

✓ Where do we make the most mistakes?

✓ Where do team members keep asking the same questions?

✓ What task would break if the current person left tomorrow?

Examples:

- Lead follow-up process
- Order dispatch flow
- Vendor payment cycle
- Client onboarding steps
- Complaint resolution

Pick the **top 3–5 processes** that cause repeated chaos.

These are your SOP priorities.

Step 2: Create a Simple SOP Format

Use this 5-part format for every SOP:

1. **SOP Name:** Client Onboarding Process

2. **Owner:** Customer Success Team
3. **When to Use:** After deal confirmation
4. **Steps (in bullets or checklist):**
   o Confirm client details in CRM
   o Send a welcome email using a template
   o Add client to WhatsApp broadcast
   o Schedule the first call
   o Share the welcome PDF + orientation video
5. **Files & Links:**
   o [Onboarding Email Template – Google Doc]
   o [Welcome PDF – Canva Link]
   o [CRM Checklist – Google Sheet]

Keep it a one-pager. Make it scannable. Use checkboxes.

Tools: Google Docs, Notion, ClickUp, Trello — or printed folders.

Step 3: Use Visuals and Videos Wherever Possible

Not everyone learns by reading.

Add:

- Screenshots of software steps
- Photos of physical process (e.g., packing)
- Short Loom videos explaining steps (2–3 mins)
- QR codes linked to video tutorials
- Flowcharts for clarity

Example:

"Scan this code to watch how we pack a bulk order the right way."

This makes SOPs **trainable without training sessions.**

Step 4: Store SOPs Where the Team Can Actually Use Them

Your SOPs should be:

- Easy to find
- Easy to open (on mobile or desktop)
- Updated regularly
- Shared with everyone who needs them

Create a central folder called **"Team Playbook"**.

Organise it by department:

📁 Sales SOPs

📁 Operations SOPs

📁 Finance SOPs

📁 HR SOPs

📁 Marketing SOPs

Use Google Drive, Notion, or a printed SOP binder with tabs, depending on what your team is comfortable with.

Step 5: Make SOPs Part of Team Habits

SOPs are not for filing. They're for use.

Make this happen by:

- ☑ Including SOP walkthroughs in onboarding

- ☑ Reviewing SOPs during monthly team reviews

- ☑ Allowing team members to suggest SOP updates

- ☑ Creating a habit of saying: *"Check the SOP first."*

- ☑ Assigning SOP champions in each department

And most importantly — **use it yourself.**

When the founder uses SOPs, the team does too.

"A business without SOPs is like a restaurant where every dish is made from memory — no consistency, scalability, and freedom."

Smart Task Management:

Know Who's Doing What, By When

Let's play a game.

Read the following and see how many sound familiar:

"He had said that he would handle it…"

"I was under the impression that you were working on it…"

"The task was assigned, but there was no follow-up."

"Who is working on this task? I don't recall."

If these sound like your daily business reality — you're not alone.

Most MSMEs run on **verbal communication, scattered WhatsApp messages, and mental task lists.** And while it may work when you're small, it **breaks completely** when you start growing.

"If tasks live in your head, they die in your execution."

In this section, we'll help you build a simple yet powerful **Task Management System** that tracks work, assigns responsibility, ensures follow-up, and creates visibility *without needing expensive software or constant nagging.*

Because when your team knows exactly **who is doing what by when** — work moves faster, smoother, and without you having to chase all the time.

The Problem: Scattered Tasks = Delayed Results

Let's say you have a 5-member team. Here's how tasks usually get assigned:

- You say something during a phone call
- A task is dropped in the middle of a WhatsApp chat
- A client calls and tells your staff something urgent
- Someone in the team says, "I will take care of that."

And then...

- No one remembers the exact deadline
- No one follows up till it's too late
- Everyone assumes someone else is doing it
- And you get pulled back in to fix, remind, or firefight

In short, **chaos disguised as "teamwork."**

The Agitation: Founder Turns into Chief Follow-Up Officer

Without task visibility:

- You start your day by asking, "What happened to that?"
- You end your day feeling like *nothing moved forward*
- Your best team members get overloaded
- Your weakest links hide behind confusion
- Work piles up — and progress slows down

The worst part?

You don't even realise how much you're chasing — until you **delegate something and still feel the need to track it personally.**

That's not delegation. That's mental outsourcing with emotional pressure. You need a better system.

The Solution: Build a Smart, Visual Task Management System

You don't need to hire a project manager.

You need **structure, visibility, and rhythm.**

Let's walk through a five-step plan you can implement this week — even if you've never used a task manager.

Step 1: Choose the Right Task Tool (Keep It Simple)

Start with what your team can actually use:

Tool	Best For	Format
Trello / ClickUp	Visual task boards, teams	Kanban (To Do / Doing / Done)
Google Sheets	Lightweight task tracking	Spreadsheet columns
WhatsApp Labels	Micro-teams or field staff	Chat tagging
Notion	Documentation + task blend	Modular format

Use a shared, **cloud-based system**. Everyone should be able to access it from a phone/laptop.

Create three basic columns:

- **To-Do** (New tasks)
- **Doing** (Currently being worked on)
- **Done** (Completed tasks)

Now, let's make this visual structure your team's new habit.

Step 2: Define the "Task Format" for Every Assignment

Train your team to use this 5-part task format:

1. **Task Name:** Clear and action-oriented
2. **Assigned To:** Person responsible (not team name)
3. **Due Date:** Exact date/time, not "ASAP"
4. **Status:** Not started, In progress, Waiting, Done
5. **Remarks:** Any dependencies, notes, or client name

Example:

Task	Assigned To	Due Date	Status	Remarks
Send revised proposal to Nisha	Amit	12 Sept	In Progress	Waiting for pricing from Vinay

No confusion and no memory games. Just **clear accountability.**

Step 3: Review Tasks on a Rhythm — Not on Mood

The best system fails without a review rhythm.

Install this into your week:

- ☑ **Daily Team Check-In (15 mins):**
  - What did you finish yesterday?
  - What are you doing today?
  - Any blockers?
- ☑ **Weekly Task Review (45 mins):**
  - Review key tasks from the week
  - Check overdue or pending work
  - Reassign or extend as needed
  - Identify what needs escalation

Use your task board as the **only agenda** for these meetings.

No distractions. No stories. Just movement.

Step 4: Track Missed Tasks and Patterns

Missed tasks aren't always bad. But **repeated misses without accountability are dangerous.**

Create a simple "Missed Task Log" to monitor patterns:

Team Member	Task Missed	Reason Given	Follow-Up Action
Preeti	Missed follow-up call	I forgot to set a reminder	Added CRM alert + note

Use this log monthly to:

- Coach underperformers
- Recognise blockers (not just blame)
- Improve clarity in assignments
- Reward consistent closers

Step 5: Create Task Transparency for the Founder

You should be able to **glance at one dashboard** and know:

- What's pending
- Who's working on what
- What's delayed
- What needs your attention

Use labels like:

- ⬤ Critical
- ◯ Delayed
- ☑ Done
- ↻ Waiting on Client

This is your *Founder Task Visibility System*. It replaces your 20 daily calls and 100 WhatsApp checks.

Peace of mind = structure + tracking.

"A task without a name, owner, and deadline is just a thought — not an action."

Bonus: Task Ownership = Team Maturity

Use this maturity ladder in your team training:

Level	Behaviour	Mindset
1	Waits to be assigned tasks	Follower
2	Completes when reminded	Dependent
3	Updates status proactively	Responsible
4	Takes ownership of results	Accountable
5	Creates and manages own tasks	Leader

Push your team to Level 3 and above. That's where **the real scale** begins.

Quick Self-Check: Is Your Task System Working?

✅ Are all team tasks captured in one visual system?

✅ Does each task have a clear owner and deadline?

✅ Do you review progress daily or weekly — not randomly?

✅ Can you, the founder, see the full picture anytime?

☑ Are delayed tasks being tracked, not forgotten?

If not, implement this now. One board, one rhythm, one result: **less chaos, more done.**

Founder Dashboards:

Take Control Without Micromanaging

You don't need to know everything.

You need to know the *right* things — at the *right* time.

Running a growing MSME often feels like juggling too many balls:

- Sales targets
- Payments stuck
- Delayed dispatches
- Team performance
- Client escalations
- Vendor follow-ups
- Marketing status

You start your day with questions like:

"What is the current status?"

"What has been completed, and what is still pending?"

"Are there any potential issues or risks developing?"

And unless you get updates from multiple people — you feel blind.

"As a founder, you don't need more data. You need smarter visibility."

This section will help you build a **Founder Dashboard**, a simple, visual tool that organises your business's key health indicators in one place.

It's not a tech tool. It's a thinking system.

Let's shift from gut feeling to informed decisions.

The Problem: No Dashboard = Daily Guesswork

Most MSME founders operate in an information fog.

- The sales team has their numbers on WhatsApp
- Ops team updates you only when something goes wrong
- Cash flow is reviewed once a month (if at all)
- You rely on memory or mood to decide on priorities

And the result?

- You make decisions based on emotion, not evidence
- You feel the need to attend every meeting to "stay updated."
- Your team overcommunicates small wins but hides key problems
- You keep reacting — instead of leading proactively

If this sounds familiar, your business is running without a **control panel.**

And every vehicle — especially one speeding up — needs a dashboard.

The Agitation: You Can't Grow What You Can't See

As your company grows:

- More people join
- More projects run in parallel
- More clients expect consistency
- More risks emerge silently

If you don't have clear visibility:

- Small issues become big fires
- You miss patterns in performance
- You lose control without even knowing it

You either spend your day chasing updates...or you end up flying blind. Neither is sustainable.

The Solution: Build a Weekly Dashboard That Guides You

A dashboard is **not** a report. It's a **real-time mirror** of your business's key health indicators.

Let's build a Founder Dashboard that helps you:

☑ Make better decisions

☑ Prioritise your time

☑ Spot problems early

☑ Empower your team

☑ Reduce dependence on memory or mood

Step 1: Identify Your Top 5–7 Business Metrics

Every business has a different DNA. But your dashboard should cover these key areas:

Category	Metric Example
Sales	Total sales (weekly/monthly)
Leads	No. of new leads + lead-to-client ratio
Operations	Orders delivered / Projects completed
Finance	Collections this week / Cash in the bank
Client Care	Complaints resolved / CSAT rating
Team	Task completion % / Attendance trends

Use metrics that are:

- Easy to update
- Actionable
- Relevant to growth

Don't clutter it with 25 KPIs. Start lean.

Step 2: Design a Simple Visual Format

Use a Google Sheet, Notion table, or basic dashboard tool.

Each row = metric

Each column = Week

Add a status colour code (Green / Yellow / Red)

Example:

Metric	Wk 1	Wk 2	Wk 3	Wk 4	Status
Sales Revenue (₹ Lakhs)	3.5	4.2	3.8	4.5	●
Collections Received	2.0	3.1	2.8	2.6	○
Orders Delivered	27	32	28	35	●
Open Complaints	3	5	4	6	●

Bonus: Add a "Top Concern of the Week" section below the table.

This gives you weekly focus, not just data.

Step 3: Assign Metric Owners

Each metric should have a **single person** who updates and explains it.

Metric	Owner
Lead Conversions	Ramesh
Collections	Asha
Complaint Status	Suraj

This creates **accountability and consistency.**

You don't have to chase people.

You review what's already been updated.

Step 4: Set a Fixed Weekly Review Slot

Don't wait for things to break.

Block 30–45 minutes **every Monday** for a dashboard review with key team members.

Agenda:

- What's on track (Green)?
- What's slipping (Yellow)?
- What needs immediate fixing (Red)?
- Is any support needed from the founder?

Use the dashboard to **drive the conversation** — not WhatsApp, not assumptions.

Step 5: Use the Dashboard to Lead — Not Control

Your dashboard is not a surveillance tool.

It's a **leadership clarity tool.**

Use it to:

- Compliment performance with facts
- Ask smarter questions

- Set weekly goals collaboratively
- Allocate resources where needed
- Spot trends early

Over time, your team will give *you* insights, not just updates.

"Dashboards turn data into direction. They help you lead with confidence, not confusion."

Bonus: Monthly Pattern Report

Once a month, ask your team to share:

✓ What improved — and why?

✓ What slipped — and how do we prevent it?

✓ What trend are they seeing that needs action?

This builds *thinking*, not just *reporting*.

Time Systems for Scale:

Free Up the Founder

What's the most overworked system in an MSME?

The **founder's brain.**

It remembers client issues, pending tasks, team problems, marketing ideas, and payments to be followed up — and still tries to stay positive, strategic, and focused.

And while you're busy putting out fires and handling urgencies, something far more dangerous is happening:

You're sacrificing the future to survive the present.

This section is about reclaiming your most limited — and most valuable — resource: **your time.**

Not with productivity hacks or motivational quotes.

But by building a **Founder's Time System** that helps you lead, think, and grow — without burning out or becoming the bottleneck.

Because scaling isn't just about what your business does.

It's about what *you stop doing*.

The Problem: No Time System = Constant Overwhelm

Here's how most founders run their day:

- Wake up and check WhatsApp
- Respond to urgent client messages
- Get dragged into team issues
- Approve small things
- Attend five calls they didn't plan
- Postpone strategic work
- End the day feeling tired but unproductive

And tomorrow? Repeat.

No planning. No protected time. There is no clarity on priorities. You may be busy, but you're not building.

You're just staying afloat.

The Agitation: Without Boundaries, Your Business Owns You

When you don't control your time:

- Urgent things always win over important ones
- Your team over-relies on your presence
- You keep deferring marketing, hiring, system-building
- You lose energy for high-leverage work
- You can't focus deeply — because something is *always* pending

And soon, your business becomes a **high-pressure job** that doesn't even give you weekends.

Scaling becomes scary, not exciting.

That's the wake-up call. Now, let's fix it.

The Solution: Install the Founder Time System

This is not about working 14 hours.

It's about **protecting your energy** and investing your hours into tasks that move the business forward—*not just keeping it running*.

Let's walk through the five pillars of your new time system.

Step 1: Design Your Ideal Week Template

You can't control every minute. But you can **pre-decide the rhythm** of your week.

Create a weekly template like this:

Time	Mon	Tue	Wed	Thu	Fri
9–10 AM	Deep Work	Deep Work	Strategy	Deep Work	Review
10–11:30 AM	Sales	Team 1:1s	Marketing	Client Call	Planning
12–1 PM	Admin	Finance	Systems	Sales	Review
2–4 PM	Execution	Execution	Thinking	Execution	Free Slot
4–5 PM	Client	Open	Open	Hiring	Wrap-up

Mark your:

- ● *Focus time* (no meetings, no calls)
- ◑ *Meeting slots* (pre-decided slots only)
- ○ *Admin & approvals*
- ● *Thinking / Planning / Vision*
- ● *Team review or mentoring*

Print this and keep it visible — on your desk, calendar, or wall.

This is your **boundary system.** Without it, others will schedule your life for you.

Step 2: Use the Weekly Rhythm Method

Every week, follow this simple 3-step cycle:

☑ **Monday Planning (20 mins)**

- Review goals
- Block key slots
- Assign big rocks

☑ **Daily Check-in (10 mins every morning)**

- Review the top 3 priorities
- Block 1–2 hours of deep work
- Push non-urgent things to appropriate slots

☑ **Friday Reflection (15 mins)**

- What got done?

- What slipped?
- What to carry forward?

Use Google Calendar or Notion. Or a simple printed Weekly Time Sheet.

Consistency matters more than format.

Step 3: Master the "Yes-Filter" for Founder Tasks

Not every task is your job.

When something comes to you, run it through this **Yes-Filter:**

Question	If YES →	If NO →
Does this need *my* brain to move forward?	Keep it	Delegate
Is it strategic, creative, or client-facing?	Prioritise	Automate/Assign
Will this matter a year from now?	Block time	Say No

Start saying:

"Let's add this to Friday's review list."

"Please update it on Trello, I'll review at 2 PM."

"This can wait — let's keep moving forward."

This removes the **reactive mode** — and makes you a better decision-maker.

Step 4: Limit Access, Not Transparency

Many founders get interrupted because they're **too available.**

Solve this with:

- Pre-fixed team check-in times (no random meetings)
- WhatsApp auto-replies: *"Please use the tracker for updates. I'll check at 4 PM."*
- Founder Office Hours — a 1-hour slot twice a week for open Q&A
- SOPs and dashboards — so your team stops asking, "What's the status?"

You're not becoming unavailable.

You're becoming **structured.**

Step 5: Protect Thinking Time at All Costs

The higher you go, the more your value lies in:

- Strategy
- Product evolution
- Culture shaping
- Hiring top talent
- Creating high-leverage ideas

These need **uninterrupted time.**

Block at least two slots per week (1–2 hours) where you:

- Turn off notifications
- Work from a quiet space
- Dive deep into solving ONE big problem
- Think about the business — not just work in it

No calls. No approvals. No multitasking.

This is where your *next breakthrough* comes from.

"A founder's calendar shows what they're building — or avoiding."

Bonus: Use the Weekly Founder Planner Tool

Create a 1-page weekly sheet:

Day	Top 3 Priorities	Blocked Time	Meetings	Notes
Monday ...		9–11 AM	2 calls	...

Use it for 21 days. You'll never go back to winging your day again.

Ownership Transfer:

Step Back Without Slipping

You've built systems.

You've brought in people.

You've created dashboards.

You've even protected your own time.

But deep down, one fear still remains:

"If I stop checking... will the work actually happen?"

This is the final frontier of scaling: learning to **delegate confiden**tly and building a business that doesn't need you for everything every day.

"Real freedom doesn't come when you do less. It comes when others do more — with ownership."

This section is about **Ownership Transfer** — shifting from founder-led to team-driven execution without losing control, quality, or speed.

Let's break the belief that *"everything will be spoiled I don't look after."* Let's replace it with a structured, tested system for empowering your team to take charge—not just follow instructions.

The Problem: Delegation Feels Risky — So It's Delayed

Here's what happens in most MSMEs:

- You hire someone to reduce your workload
- You explain the task, sometimes twice
- You get a poor result or missed deadline
- You get frustrated
- You say, *"Leave it, I'll do it myself."*

And the cycle repeats.

You're not a control freak. You just care about results.

But without a framework for ownership, **your team becomes dependent, not decisive.**

The Agitation: You Stay Stuck in the Founder's Trap

When ownership is missing:

- You're the go-to person for every decision
- Work only moves when you approve it
- Clients insist on talking to *you*
- Team members hesitate to take bold steps
- Every small task drags your attention

And the moment you go on leave, growth pauses.

This is not just inefficient. It's dangerous.

Because your business can't scale **if it can't survive your absence.**

The Solution: Build the Ownership Transfer System

You don't delegate to remove tasks.

You delegate to **grow people** and **scale outcomes** — without compromising quality.

Let's walk through a 5-part system to shift real ownership — not just handover checklists.

Step 1: Define Levels of Ownership

Start by creating clarity on what "ownership" even means.

Use this **Ownership Ladder**:

Level	Description	Example
1	Do only when told	"Call this client now."
2	Complete assigned tasks	"Here's the list. Finish it today."
3	Take the initiative on known processes	"I've followed up, and here's the status."
4	Own outcomes with regular updates	"Target achieved — reporting weekly."
5	Drive growth and suggest improvements	"I've redesigned the process for better speed."

Your goal is to consistently move each team member from **Level 2 to Level 4**.

Step 2: Create an Ownership Handover Map

Ownership is not transferred in one sentence.

It's handed over in phases.

Use this **4-Stage Handover Path:**

Stage	Description
◆ Shadowing	They watch you do it
◆ Assisted Run	They do it with you watching
◆ Independent	They do it alone + send you updates
◆ Leadership	They improve it and coach others

Create this map for each key process or role.

Example:

"Client Onboarding Process"

- Week 1–2: Shadow calls and documentation
- Week 3: Do onboarding with a checklist; you review
- Week 4–5: Handle end-to-end, you get summary
- Week 6+: Fully independent; only escalations reported

This ensures **quality doesn't drop as ownership rises.**

Step 3: Set Decision Boundaries (Not Just Task Lists)

F founders don't delegate *because "He will make a wrong decision."* Solve this with **Decision Boundaries.**

Create a simple chart like this:

Situation	Team can...	Must escalate if...
Delay < 2 days	Inform client	Delay > 2 days
Discount < 5%	Apply directly	>5% needs approval
Vendor issue (non-urgent)	Resolve independently	Impacts deadline or quality
Client unhappy after 2nd follow-up	Escalate to founder	–

This gives freedom **with guardrails.**

Step 4: Build a Weekly Ownership Review Rhythm

Every Friday, spend 30–45 mins with key team members to ask:

- What did you own this week?
- What result came out of it?
- Where did you feel stuck?
- What can be improved in your process?
- What's your next goal — without me pushing it?

This builds a culture of **reflection, reporting, and responsibility.**

Use a simple **Ownership Journal Template**:

Team Member	Area Owned	Result This Week	Blockers	Next Goal
Priya	Dispatch Process	100% on-time	One vendor delayed	Improve packing quality

Over time, the team mindset shifts from *"Tell me what to do"* to *"Here's what I'm driving."*

Step 5: Celebrate Ownership Publicly

What gets praised gets repeated. Create micro-culture rituals:

- "Owner of the Week" shoutouts
- A whiteboard listing team wins
- Notes from clients displayed on the team wall
- Spot bonuses for autonomous decision-making
- Recognition in team meetings for those who take charge

Ownership is not a task. It's a **team identity.**

When you celebrate it — others follow.

"Delegation is not giving away control. It's growing new leaders."

Bonus Tool: The Ownership Transfer Canvas

Create a 1-page handover document for each critical process:

Process Name	Owner	Handover Stage	Decision Limits	Update Rhythm
Client Onboarding	Asha	Independent	Escalate beyond ₹10K delay	Weekly Summary
Vendor Payments	Anuj	Assisted Run	Over ₹50K approval needed	Daily by 4 PM

Keep it visible in team folders. Review monthly.

Watch ownership evolve — visibly.

Quick Self-Check: Are You Transferring Ownership or Just Tasks?

☑ Do team members own results — not just to-dos?

☑ Are decision boundaries clearly defined?

☑ Do you have a handover rhythm or canvas?

☑ Are you tracking weekly ownership wins?

☑ Are you stepping back — without quality slipping?

If not, start with one person, process, and rhythm.

Build from there.

Final Word on Systems for Scaling

You've now completed the scale foundation:

- SOPs
- Task Management
- Dashboards
- Time Systems
- Ownership Transfer

This is not just structure. It's **freedom.**

Freedom to grow, innovate, and breathe — without your business falling apart.

You've gone from *a daily hustle* to a *scalable engine.*

Next, let's turn this engine into a business that attracts talent, retains clients, and — maybe — even prepares for IPO-level readiness.

Let's step into your next-level business chapters. You're ready.

Chapter 10: The Brand Power Play

Build Perception That Multiplies Value

You've put in the hard work.

You've solved sales, retained customers, built systems, trained your team, and freed yourself from the day-to-day.

But as you grow, you'll soon realise:

"It's not enough to be great — you must also be seen as great."

This is where many MSMEs stumble.

They build strong products.

They run stable operations.

They serve loyal customers.

But when a new client Googles them, they find... nothing.

When a talented professional check their LinkedIn... it's outdated.

When an investor hears their pitch... it sounds small.

And in today's hyper-visible world, **perception becomes part of your product.**

"Brand is not lipstick. It's the face your business wears in public."

This chapter is about building that face — not for vanity, but for **value.**

Because the businesses that attract better clients, stronger talent, and premium partnerships... are the ones that *feel trustworthy* from the outside.

The Problem: MSMEs Confuse Branding with Design

Most small and medium business owners think branding means:

- A new logo
- A visiting card
- A colour palette
- A company brochure
- A one-time post on Instagram

And so, they delay it.

"Let's do branding later... once we're bigger."

But branding isn't about decoration.

It's about **building trust at scale.**

It's the reason a stranger says, *"You look credible."*

It's why a client says, *"You feel like a premium company."*

It's the reason a potential hire says, *"I want to work with them."*

Without that trust, you remain invisible — no matter how good your work is.

The Agitation: Without Brand, You Stay a Vendor — Not a Valued Partner

Here's what happens to MSMEs who don't build a visible, consistent brand:

- Prospective clients bargain on price — because they don't see your value
- Your best work stays hidden — because no one showcases it properly
- Good team members hesitate to join — because your company seems "too small."
- You lose deals — not because you're worse, but because you *look* less prepared
- Investors skip you — not because of your numbers, but because your pitch lacks story and structure

This is not a marketing gap.

It's a **brand leadership gap.**

And it silently limits your growth.

The Solution: Build the Brand as a Strategic Asset — Not a Side Project

This chapter will show you how to build a brand like a pro—even if you're small, new to digital, or on a tight budget.

Not with flashy design agencies.

But with clarity, consistency, and **controlled visibility** that builds over time.

Let's preview what you'll learn ahead.

10.1: Brand is Not a Logo – It's the Promise You Keep

We'll begin by **redefining the brand** for MSMEs.

You'll learn:

- The difference between logo, marketing, and brand
- Why "consistency" builds more trust than any ad
- How to identify the promises you want to be known for
- What your brand should *feel like* to clients, vendors, and team

You'll come away with a personal **Brand Clarity Canvas**™ that you can use to brief designers, write posts, or pitch clients — all from a place of **authentic identity.**

10.2: Positioning to Stand Out – Become the Obvious Choice

In this section, we'll work on your **positioning.**

You'll learn:

- How to craft your "Category of One" message
- How to avoid being compared on price
- How to answer, "Why you and not someone else?"
- How to write an elevator pitch that sticks in the mind

Using proven templates and exercises, you'll develop a clear **Positioning Statement** that your sales team, social media, and website can align with.

This is how you become the **obvious, not the cheapest** choice.

10.3: Online Presence Playbook – Win Trust Before the First Call

Before anyone speaks to you — they search you.

This section will help you create a **Minimum Viable Online Presence** using:

- A lean, well-written website
- Updated Google Business profile
- Founder's optimised LinkedIn
- WhatsApp Business profile with auto-responses

- Case studies, testimonials, and visual proof of work

You'll learn to use tools like Canva, Wix, and ChatGPT to build trust — *even before the first call happens.*

Because in today's world, **online = first impression.**

10.4: Talent Magnetism – Make People Want to Work with You

The brand isn't just for clients. It's also your secret weapon for **attracting talent.**

Here you'll learn:

- How to write job posts that inspire — not bore
- How to showcase your team culture and values
- What to put on your Careers page or LinkedIn to excite candidates
- How to tell your founder story in a way that builds loyalty

Because the best people don't just want a job.

They want to **belong** to a mission.

Let's help your brand speak to them.

10.5: Investor-Ready Storytelling – Pitch with Power

Finally, we'll bring it all together with your **narrative.**

In this section, you'll learn:

- How to present your growth story in investor language
- What goes into a 5-slide pitch deck for funding or partnerships?
- How to frame your market, moat, and momentum
- What to say — and what to *stop* saying — when presenting your company

Even if you're not raising funds today, this clarity helps in:

✅ Getting better clients

✅ Forming partnerships

✅ Preparing for IPO

✅ Earning long-term trust

Because investors don't back spreadsheets.

They back **stories with structure.**

Build a Brand That Commands Respect

✅ So clients choose you — not compare you

☑ So team members grow with you — not leave for better-looking companies

☑ So you scale value — not just revenue

☑ So you get invited to rooms where pricing is not the only criteria

This is not about image.

This is about **business positioning.**

Let's help your MSME look, feel, and *lead* like the company it's becoming—not the company it used to be.

Brand is Not a Logo:

It's the Promise You Keep

What comes to your mind when you hear the word "brand"?

A logo?

A social media posts?

A shiny brochure?

If you nodded at any of those — you're not alone.

But here's the hard truth:

Your logo is not your brand. Your design is not your identity.

Your brand is the **feeling** someone gets when they think about your business.

It's the **promise** your company makes — and keeps — at every touchpoint.

It's how people describe you when you're not in the room.

And for MSMEs like yours, building a strong brand isn't about flashy ads.

It's about **consistent trust.**

The Problem: Most MSMEs Treat Branding as Decoration

In most small and mid-sized businesses, branding is often seen as:

- An "extra expense."
- A marketing department activity
- Something that only matters for large companies
- A one-time exercise when launching a website or packaging

As a result:

- Business cards are printed... but never used
- Websites exist... but aren't updated for years
- Logos look good... but mean nothing
- Clients buy... but don't remember

And yet, the founder wonders: *"Why are people not referring us?"*

Or *"Why don't we stand out?"*

Because in the absence of branding, **you become invisible.**

The Agitation: In a Crowded Market, No Brand = No Value

Let's look at what happens when branding is weak or unclear:

- Clients compare you purely on price — because they can't perceive your value

• Your team doesn't know what your business stands for — so they can't communicate it

• You struggle to differentiate — even when your quality is better

• You lose the attention of decision-makers — because nothing about your business is memorable

• You miss out on partnerships, referrals, and opportunities — because no one thinks of you first

Your business may be excellent, but **without brand clarity, you stay underestimated.**

And that invisibility hurts more than rejection.

The Solution: Build Your Brand on Promises, Not Pixels

A real brand isn't built in Photoshop. It's built in the **hearts and minds** of people who experience you.

Let's explore five building blocks to start shaping your MSME's brand — from the inside out.

1. Define Your Core Promise

Ask yourself: *"What do I want my clients to always trust me for?"*

It could be:

- "We make your business look world-class."
- "We always deliver before the deadline."
- "We treat small clients like big ones."
- "We bring innovation to traditional industries."

> • "We remove the headache — not just deliver a product."

This is not a tagline. It's your **brand promise.** Everything else — your communication, service, and packaging — must align with this promise.

2. Discover How People Currently Perceive You

Before you decide on your brand, find out what it *is*.

Ask 5–10 of your clients, vendors, and team:

> • "When you think of our business, what words come to mind?"
> • "Why do you trust us?"
> • "Why did you choose us over others?"
> • "Where do you think we can improve our image?"

This will reveal your **current brand perception**.

Sometimes, the gap between what you think and what they feel is huge — and that's where your work begins.

3. Craft Your Brand Pillars

Every strong brand stands on 3–5 key **pillars** — values or attributes you consistently embody.

For example:

Brand Pillar	What It Means in Practice
Reliability	Delivering on time every time
Simplicity	Easy onboarding, clear communication, no jargon
Innovation	Regularly improving processes and products
Personal Touch	Founder calls new clients personally, birthday wishes
Transparency	Clear pricing, no hidden clauses

Write your own. Share them with your team. Review them quarterly.

These are not just words — they become your **operating principles.**

4. Express Your Brand Consistently Across Touchpoints

Once your brand promise and pillars are clear.

Show it everywhere.

• Website: Is the messaging aligned? Does it feel premium or generic?

• Proposals: Do they reflect your attention to detail and professionalism?

• WhatsApp/Email: Does your tone match your brand (e.g., warm, formal, efficient)?

• Office Environment: Does it reflect your values (e.g., discipline, creativity, warmth)?

- Delivery Experience: Does it *feel* different from competitors?

Consistency creates **recognition**, and recognition leads to **trust.**

Every touchpoint is either building or breaking your brand.

5. Document It All in a Brand Clarity Sheet

Create a one-page internal document called your **Brand Clarity Sheet.**

Element	Your Brand Example
Brand Promise	We make scaling simple for SME founders.
Brand Tone	Expert + Warm + Direct
Brand Pillars	Clarity, Accountability, Founder-Friendliness
Preferred Colours	Navy Blue, Grey, Gold
Visual Style	Clean, Minimal, Structured
Founder Voice	Strategic, Empathetic, Action-Oriented

This becomes your **branding compass** — for content, hiring, communication, and design.

Use it to brief vendors, onboard team members, and guide marketing.

"People don't remember what you said. They remember how you made them feel."

Your brand is the feeling you create — **consistently.**

Quick Self-Check: Are You Brand-Ready?

☑ Have you defined your core brand promise — in one clear sentence?

☑ Do you know what clients and vendors say about your brand now?

☑ Are your brand pillars visible in daily operations?

☑ Is your online/offline presence consistent with your identity?

☑ Do you have a Brand Clarity Sheet for your team?

If not, take a few hours this week to build it.

Because the world doesn't choose the best product.

It chooses the **most trusted, visible, and consistent brand.**

Let's make *your MSME* that brand.

Positioning to Stand Out:

Become the Obvious Choice

In every market, in every city, in every industry — some businesses are:

- Cheaper
- Bigger
- Older
- Louder

But still… some brands get picked first.

Why?

Because they've mastered the art of **positioning.**

"Positioning is the space your business owns in the customer's mind."

It's not about what you *do.*

It's about what people *think you do best.*

And more importantly — what they **remember** and **repeat** to others.

In a world where everyone is shouting, "Buy from us!" strong positioning whispers,

"We're exactly what you're looking for."

The Problem: Most MSMEs Sound the Same

Let's say you're at a trade show or browsing company websites.

Here's what you see:

- "We believe in quality and service."
- "Customer satisfaction is our goal."
- "We provide end-to-end solutions."
- "Trusted by many clients across India."

And you wonder: *"So what? How are you different?"*

The hard truth?

Most MSMEs blend into the background — not because they're bad, but because they're **boring.**

If your messaging doesn't make people pause and say, "Tell me more,"

you're not positioned — you're just present.

The Agitation: Poor Positioning = Price Wars, Delayed Sales & Lost Deals

Without sharp positioning:

- Clients take longer to decide — because they're unsure of your value
- You get compared on price — because there's no perceived difference

- Your sales team struggles to explain *why you're better*
- Referrals don't work — because people don't know what to say about you
- Your website and brochures feel flat — because there's no unique story

Even worse, your **best potential clients go to weaker competitors** who sound clearer.

Let's change that.

The Solution: Build Positioning That Sticks, Sells & Scales

Powerful positioning does three things:

1. **Clarifies** what you stand for
2. **Differentiates** you from alternatives
3. **Magnifies** your perceived value

Let's explain how you can build yours — with examples, tools, and real-world context.

Step 1: Identify Your "Only We" Claim

Start with this question:

"What do we do differently, better, or more consistently than 90% of our competitors?"

Frame it using the **Only We Statement**:

"We are the only [category] that [unique benefit or promise] for [specific customer type]."

Examples:

- "We are the only digital signage company that delivers within 48 hours across 7 Indian cities — guaranteed."
- "We are the only accounting firm focused 100% on export-based MSMEs."
- "We are the only packaging vendor in Jaipur offering biodegradable luxury boxes under ₹20/unit."

Even if you're not the only one — the *first to say it clearly* owns the space.

Step 2: Nail Your Elevator Pitch

Most founders say:

"We do printing, designing, packaging, and logistics services for all industries."

That's not a pitch. That's a **confusion bomb.**

Use this simple **3-part Elevator Pitch Framework**:

"We help [target audience] solve [specific problem] using [your core offer or secret sauce], so they can [benefit/result]."

Examples:

- "We help restaurants struggling with poor lighting install elegant, low-cost ambience systems in under 7 days — so they attract more walk-ins and Instagram posts."

- "We help B2B companies reduce their digital marketing wastage by running ROI-focused LinkedIn campaigns — even if they've never run ads."

Keep it under 30 seconds. Test it at events. Train your sales team to use it.

Put it on your homepage and proposal cover.

Step 3: Create a Positioning Comparison Grid

Help your clients see the difference **visually.**

Use a simple table like this:

Feature/Benefit	You	Competitor A	Competitor B
Delivery Time	48 hours	4–7 days	Uncertain
Specialisation	Only B2B	Mixed clients	Mostly retail
Post-Sale Support	Dedicated rep	Hotline only	No follow-up
Customisation Level	High	Medium	Low
Eco-Friendly Option	Yes	No	No

This becomes your sales weapon. It gives your prospect **a reason to pay more — or say yes faster.**

Step 4: Position by Category — Not Just Product

If your product sounds like everyone else's, change the *category*.

Instead of saying, "We make corrugated boxes," say:

"We are a sustainable packaging partner for craft D2C brands in India."

Instead of "We do HR consulting," say:

"We build internal teams for scaling startups — without costly hiring agencies."

Instead of "We're a garments manufacturer," say:

"We help premium brands scale without inventory headaches — with our ready-to-label collection."

The world doesn't remember products.

It remembers **positioned problems with clear solutions.**

Step 5: Validate with Real Clients — Then Refine

Once you've created your new positioning:

- Test it in a few sales calls
- Ask past clients, "Does this describe what we did for you?"
- Put it on your WhatsApp Business profile
- Run a simple LinkedIn post with it — see the reactions
- Use it as the opening line of your next email campaign

Positioning is not carved in stone. It's shaped in conversations.

Refine it every 90 days. Own it every day.

Quick Self-Check: Are You Positioned to Stand Out?

☑ Can you explain your value clearly in 30 seconds?

☑ Do your website and proposals say what makes you different?

☑ Does your sales team have a pitch that creates curiosity?

☑ Can clients explain what you do — in their own words?

☑ Are you being compared on value, not just price?

If not, spend the next few hours crafting your **Only We Statement** and testing your elevator pitch.

It will change how people see you — and how you see your own business.

Online Presence Playbook:

Win Trust Before the First Call

Imagine a potential client who hears about your business from a referral or a WhatsApp group.

What do they do next?

They Google your name.

They check your website (if you have one).

They look at your LinkedIn.

They browse your WhatsApp Business profile.

Maybe even your Instagram, YouTube, or recent posts.

Now ask yourself:

"What do they see… and what does it say about me?"

Because before they call you, they've already made a **mental note**:

- "This business feels serious."
- "Looks small, but interesting."
- "They're probably expensive."
- "Hmm, can't find much… maybe not for us."
- "Wow, they work with businesses like ours!"

This is your **online brand audit.**

"Today, trust is built in the digital world before it's built-in person."

This section will show you how to build a lean but powerful **online presence** — even if you're not tech-savvy or active on social media.

Because in today's business world, **your first impression is digital.**

The Problem: MSMEs Underinvest in Digital Identity

Most growing MSMEs fall into one of three categories:

- No digital presence at all — "We work on referrals only."
- Outdated presence — "We made our site in 2015."
- Random presence — "Sometimes we post something on Instagram."

The result?

- You lose high-quality leads who silently check and bounce
- You get compared to more polished competitors
- You miss opportunities from decision-makers looking for credibility
- Your sales team has to work harder to "prove" your value
- Potential talent skips you — because you *look* small

A weak digital presence is not just a marketing gap — it's a **trust gap.**

The Agitation: Without Online Presence, You Look Invisible or Insecure

Ask yourself honestly:

- If a top client Googled your name, would they be impressed?
- If an investor checked your LinkedIn, would they want a meeting?
- If a vendor searched your website, would they feel confident supplying you?
- If a future employee checked your brand, would they see a career — or just a job?

If your answer is "no" or "not sure," you operate with a **hidden disadvantage.**

You might be exceptional in real life — but you're **forgettable online.**

Let's fix that.

The Solution: Build a Lean, Professional, Low-Maintenance Online Presence

You don't need to go viral.

You don't need to hire an agency.

You don't even need to post daily.

You must look like a **modern, serious, and trusted brand** — in 5 key places.

Let's break them down one by one.

1. Build a Simple, Effective Website

Your website is not for traffic. It's for **trust.**

A good MSME website has just five sections:

Section	Purpose
Home	Clear value proposition + CTA
About Us	The story, values, founder message
Services/Products	What you do — explained simply
Testimonials/Clients	Visual proof and trust indicators
Contact	WhatsApp, phone, Google Maps, email

Tools: Wix, Webflow, Squarespace, WordPress (for more control).

Time to build: 3–5 days max.

Budget: ₹5,000–₹25,000 if done smartly.

Put your logo, positioning line, client logos, and contact details — all in one scroll.

2. Optimise Your Google Business Profile

This is *the most* underrated MSME growth tool.

☑ Claim your business on Google My Business

☑ Add the correct location, photos, and services

☑ Add business hours, website, and CTA

Why it matters:

- You show up when someone searches your name
- You rank in local searches ("packaging vendor near me")
- You look real, visible, and trusted

And yes — it's free.

3. Upgrade Your WhatsApp Business Profile

Most MSMEs already use WhatsApp. But few use it **as a brand.** Here's what to set up:

Element	What to Do
Display Picture	Your logo or clear brand image
Business Name	Company name (not "Available"!)
About Section	One-liner value statement
Quick Replies	Pre-set answers to common queries
Catalogue	Photos + pricing (even if PDF)
Auto Reply	"Thanks for reaching out; we'll get back shortly."

This turns WhatsApp into your **digital front desk.**

4. Fix Your Founder & Company LinkedIn

People trust people — not just companies.

What to do:

- Optimise your founder profile (headline, summary, logo, banner)
- Add key clients, achievements, press, or posts
- Create a company page with the logo, one-line intro, and website link
- Post 1–2 updates per month: projects, behind-the-scenes, recognitions

No dancing reels. There are no "Good Morning" quotes. Just **clean, relevant visibility.**

5. Show Proof with Visuals – Once a Week

Build a simple "Digital Proof Bank":

- Before/after photos
- Happy customer selfies
- Installation or delivery shots
- Certificates, awards, coverage
- Founder photos in action
- Snippets of thank-you messages

Post one every week on:

 LinkedIn

☑ WhatsApp Status

☑ Instagram (optional)

This creates a **slow drip of trust** in your network.

Talent Magnetism:

Make People Want to Work with You

You've worked hard to build a strong product.

You've created systems, structure, and stability.

You're visible online, and your messaging is sharp.

But here's the next big challenge:

"Can you attract and retain people who help you grow — without handholding or headache?"

In most MSMEs, team building is reactive:

- "Someone left… now we need to hire."
- "We posted a job… no one good applied."
- "We hired someone… but they left in 3 months."
- "We train them… but they're not serious."
- "We can't afford experienced people right now."

It feels like a never-ending loop.

"If clients build revenue, your team builds freedom."

This section will help you build **Talent Magnetism** — the ability to attract better people faster and keep them longer — *not because of salary alone* but because of your **brand and culture.**

The Problem: MSMEs Are Not Seen as 'Aspirational Employers'

Let's be honest.

Most job seekers, especially young talent, dream of:

- Big brands
- Startup unicorns
- Tech companies
- Corporate training programs
- Fancy offices and perks

Meanwhile, MSMEs are often viewed as:

- Risky
- Unstructured
- Low-paying
- Boring
- "Just a job" — not a career

Even when your company is amazing, you're judged by:

- Your outdated website
- Poorly written job descriptions
- No social media presence
- No founder visibility
- No clear career path

So you get:

- Average applications
- High dropouts
- Talent you can't fully trust or train

The Agitation: Without Talent Magnetism, You Stay Trapped in a Hiring Spiral

What happens when your brand doesn't attract talent?

- You always hire in panic mode
- You settle for "whoever is available."
- You spend weeks training — only to start over
- You can't delegate key work
- You stay stuck in execution
- And eventually, you **burn out**

Without great people, you can't grow.

And without brand magnetism, **great people won't find you.**

The Solution: Build a Brand That Talent Wants to Join — and Stay With

You don't need to become Google or Tata to attract serious team members.

You need to **stand out in your category** — as a company that's:

☑ Clear in its values

☑ Serious about growth

☑ Invested in people

☑ Visible online

☑ Run by a founder with a vision

Let's now build your **Talent Magnetism System** — step by step.

Step 1: Craft a Powerful Employer Message

Ask yourself:

"Why should someone join me — and stay for 3+ years?"

Write a 2–3-line **Employer Pitch** you can use in job posts, LinkedIn, interviews, and onboarding.

Example:

"We're a fast-growing MSME that helps Indian retailers modernise their packaging. We're not a corporate — but we offer serious learning, real responsibility, and the chance to grow with us as we expand into three new cities this year."

Your employer's message should answer the following:

- What you do
- Who you serve
- Where you're going
- Why the role matters
- What's in it for the candidate

Step 2: Show Your Culture — Don't Just Talk About It

You don't need an HR department to build culture.

You need **rituals, rhythm, and visibility.**

Ways to show your work culture online:

Format	Idea
LinkedIn Post	Behind the scenes of a team project
WhatsApp Status	"Happy Work Anniversary" shoutout
Instagram Stories	Friday team lunch or onboarding moment
Blog/Article	"What I Learned in My First 30 Days at [Your Brand]"

This helps you build a **reputation beyond salary.**

Step 3: Fix Your Job Post — Make It Exciting, Not Generic

Most MSME job ads are dull:

"Wanted: Admin executive. 2–3 years' experience. Fluent in English. Salary as per industry norms."

Here's how to upgrade it:

1. **Start with a hook:**

2. "Want to be part of a fast-growing team where your ideas actually matter?"

3. **Describe the mission:**

4. "We help FMCG brands get shelf-ready in 72 hours — and we're growing 3x yearly."

5. **Highlight the role impact:**

6. "You'll work directly with the founder to set up vendor systems that run without micromanagement."

7. **Show growth:**

8. "We've promoted three juniors to senior roles in 12 months. If you're ambitious, you'll love it here."

9. **Use visual aids:**

10. Add a video or image of your office, team, or workspace.

Great people respond to **great energy.**

Step 4: Onboard Like You Mean It

First impressions last — especially for new hires.

Create a simple **Onboarding Starter Kit:**

- Founder welcome video (or personal call)
- Company overview PDF
- Org chart + who to go to for what
- 30-day learning plan
- Culture Do's & Don'ts sheet
- Weekly check-in form

Onboarding shows that you're **serious about people.** And serious companies attract serious talent.

Step 5: Share Team Wins Publicly

People want to work where others are **valued.**

Ways to do this:

- "Team Member of the Month" posts
- Celebrate certifications, promotions, anniversaries
- Showcase real project wins
- Let team members post stories from their side

You'll attract better applicants, and your current team will **stay with you longer.**

"Talent doesn't follow job descriptions. It follows energy, vision, and respect."

Investor-Ready Storytelling:

Pitch with Power

You've got a product that works.

A team that delivers.

Clients who trust you.

And a brand that's starting to shine.

Now comes the next level.

"Can you explain your business in a way that gets people to bet on you?"

Whether you're speaking to investors, strategic partners, grant committees, or future co-founders — you're not just presenting numbers.

You're telling a **story.**

Because what gets funded, remembered, or shared isn't always the most profitable company — it's the most **compellingly positioned company.**

"Facts tell. Stories sell. But investor-ready stories raise."

In this chapter, you'll learn how to craft your MSME's growth story so clearly and powerfully that the world sees what you've built — and believes in where you're going.

The Problem: Founders Talk but Don't Pitch

Most MSME founders, when asked "What do you do?" respond with:

- "We manufacture corrugated boxes since 2011…"
- "We provide custom software for educational institutions…"
- "We are into packaging, printing, and promotional materials…"

It's descriptive. It's accurate. But it's **not persuasive.**

Investor-ready storytelling is not about giving *more data*.

It's about **shaping perception.**

A weak pitch leaves people saying:

- "Hmm… okay."
- "Interesting. Send me more details."
- "Sounds like a lot of other businesses."

And you lose the moment — not because you're not worth it, but because you **couldn't convey it.**

The Agitation: Weak Story = Lost Opportunities

Let's say:

- You meet an angel investor at a conference
- A startup accelerator invites you for a shortlisting round
- A banker asks for a business overview

- You want to post a funding announcement online
- You're on a stage explaining your SME's journey

What happens if your story is:

- Confusing
- Generic
- Full of jargon
- Founder-centric (not client- or market-centric)
- Missing the 'so what' factor

You get nods — but no follow-ups.

You lose funding, partnerships, and credibility—not because you lack performance… but because you lack **presentation.**

The Solution: Build a Pitch That Inspires Confidence

You don't need to become a TED speaker or startup founder.

You need to tell your MSME story in a way that feels:

☑ Confident

☑ Data-backed

☑ Forward-looking

☑ Client-centric

☑ Visionary

Let's now build your **Investor-Ready Story Structure** — step by step.

Step 1: Craft the 5-Slide Narrative Framework

Whether it's a 2-minute conversation or a 10-minute presentation, use this core format:

Slide/Section	What to Include
1. The Problem	What pain does your customer face?
2. Your Solution	What unique value do you offer?
3. Your Traction	Key milestones, revenue growth, repeat clients
4. Your Vision	Where are you going? How big can this get?
5. The Ask	What are you looking for — money, partners, support?

Example Pitch Opener:

"In India, over 80% of tier-2 city retailers struggle with poor-quality, delayed packaging vendors. We've solved that with a plug-and-play solution that delivers within 72 hours and offers eco-friendly, custom-designed boxes. In just 18 months, we've served 400+ clients and crossed ₹2.1 Cr in revenue. Now, we're expanding into three more cities and looking for strategic capital to build regional hubs and a tech-enabled ordering platform."

Short. Sharp. Structured. Strong.

Step 2: Add Data Without Drowning in It

Investors love numbers. But not **every** number.

Focus on these six metrics:

Metric	Why It Matters
Revenue Trend (last 3 yrs)	Shows growth potential
Customer Retention Rate	Indicates client satisfaction
Gross Margin %	Reveals business sustainability
TAM/SAM (Market Size)	Validates long-term opportunity
Order Fulfilment Time	Shows operational strength
Founder Skin in the Game	Indicates seriousness and commitment

Add visuals:

Use bar charts, milestone timelines, and before/after customer quotes.

Keep your deck at 8–10 slides. Clarity wins over clutter.

Step 3: Tell the Origin Story with Emotion, Not Ego

Don't start with:

"We started in 2014 with two partners and now have 18 employees..."

Start with:

"I ran a gift business and faced the same frustration — unreliable box vendors. I realised that if I had this problem, so did thousands of other D2C founders. That's when the idea of [Your MSME] was born."

Every investor wants to know:

- Why **you**?
- Why **this**?
- Why **now**?

Let them see the human spark behind the machine.

Step 4: Show Your Moat — What Makes You Hard to Beat

Answer the hidden question:

"What stops someone else from copying you tomorrow?"

Ways to answer:

- Proprietary process or sourcing network
- Client relationships in high-trust categories
- Location dominance
- Speed or customisation
- Strong referral engine
- Ecosystem play (e.g., bundled services)

Show them how you've **earned** your growth — not stumbled into it.

Step 5: Close with Vision + Action

Paint a picture of the next 3 years:

- "Our goal is to become India's top custom-packaging platform for D2C brands."
- "We plan to launch three regional hubs, expand to 100 cr topline, and serve 5,000 clients."
- "We're building a team that can run without the founder — and plan to prepare for SME IPO readiness by 2028."

Then ask with clarity:

"We're looking to raise ₹1.5 Cr in strategic capital to build our warehouse, strengthen our tech, and scale our team."

"Investors don't just bet on ideas — they bet on founders who can tell a story that feels real, ready, and worth backing."

Bonus: Storytelling Toolkit for MSMEs

- **Investor One-Pager Template**
- **Pitch Deck Template (10-slide format)**
- **Founder Pitch Script (2-minute version)**
- **Vision Board Format (PDF for internal alignment)**

Use these to align your team, partners, and future investors.

Chapter 11: IPO Readiness

Scale with Discipline, Confidence & Visibility

You've come a long way.

Your sales engine is humming.

Your systems are structured.

Your team is stabilising.

Your brand is building equity.

And your growth story is finally worth talking about.

Now comes the million-dollar question — sometimes quite literally:

"Can your business stand tall under scrutiny — from investors, banks, partners, or even the public market?"

Because at some point, every ambitious MSME reaches a turning point.

You no longer want to be just profitable.

You want to be *fundable.*

You want scale — not just stability.

You want to be seen as a **serious, structured, future-ready company.**

This is where **IPO readiness** becomes your next big shift.

"IPO readiness is not about going public tomorrow. It's about building a business that's worthy of it — today."

This chapter will walk you through installing the discipline, systems, governance, and visibility needed to make your business **IPO-capable—even if you don't plan to list right away.**

Preparation gives you **options**—to raise capital, attract premium clients, earn supplier trust, or even invite strategic investors.

The Problem: MSMEs Confuse IPO With Just Profitability

In conversations with MSME founders, we often hear:

- "IPO? We're not that big yet."
- "Let me touch ₹100 Cr, then we'll think about it."
- "We're not tech or VC-funded. IPO is not for us."
- "We'll do it when we're ready."

But here's the truth:

IPO readiness has little to do with size — and everything to do with structure.

A company doing ₹40–50 Cr revenue with 15% EBITDA and clean books is **more IPO-ready** than a ₹120 Cr firm with messy books, founder dependency, and zero reporting culture.

So, the real problem?

☞ MSMEs delay preparation — and then panic when opportunity knocks.

Whether it's:

- A sudden investor inquiry
- A government incentive tied to financial disclosure
- A banker asking for board meeting minutes
- Or a merchant banker scouting for SME IPO candidates

...they're caught off guard.

By the time they realise what's required, it's already late.

The Agitation: When You're Not Ready, You Miss the Window

Here's what happens when you're not IPO-prepped:

- You struggle to present your numbers clearly
- Your systems fall apart under due diligence

- Your business looks founder-dependent — not process-driven
- You fail the governance test — no board minutes, no internal audit trails
- Your financials raise red flags — no cost controls, no margin tracking
- You can't inspire confidence — because everything feels makeshift

And here's the punchline:

You may be performing well — but the world **can't trust you yet.**

Not because you're dishonest.

But because your **structure doesn't support scrutiny.**

And that's where the scale begins to plateau.

The Solution: Start Preparing Like You'll List in 3 Years — Even If You Don't

This chapter is not about pushing you into an IPO.

It's about helping you:

☑ Install financial discipline

☑ Run your business like a listed company

☑ Clean up governance and reporting

☑ Become founder-independent

☑ Build a narrative investors and partners believe in

☑ And keep the **option** to go public open — on *your terms*

Let's give you the roadmap — five practical, founder-friendly sections.

11.1: What IPO Readiness Really Means – More Than Just Financials

We'll start by busting the biggest myths around IPOs.

You'll learn:

- What exchanges, merchant bankers, and investors actually look for
- The difference between financial strength vs. financial *visibility*
- Why team, governance, predictability, and founder role clarity matter
- And how IPO readiness helps even if you never go public

This section sets the foundation — and the mindset.

11.2: Clean Up Operations, Governance & Reporting

Here, we'll build your internal hygiene.

You'll get a blueprint to:

- Set up structured board meetings
- Maintain statutory registers
- Install reporting dashboards
- Create process ownership
- Document decisions and policies
- And prepare audit trails that survive scrutiny

Governance is not bureaucracy — it's **trust infrastructure.**

11.3: Build a Financial & Compliance Culture

Numbers speak louder than claims.

This section teaches you to:

- Track monthly MIS and key ratios
- Maintain clean P&L, balance sheet, and cash flow
- Integrate cost centres, project profitability, and vendor tracking
- Avoid last-minute CA rushes — and think like a CFO
- Create a compliance calendar (GST, ROC, PF, TDS, etc.)

This is where *professionalism replaces jugaad.*

11.4: Leadership, Board, & Systems That Impress Investors

Now, we polish your people and structure.

You'll learn:

- How to build a board (even if informal at first)
- Which roles should shift from founder to team
- How to showcase advisory support
- Why succession planning increases valuation
- And what investors look for in people — not just products

Investors back vision — but they bet on **systems and leadership.**

11.5: Create Your IPO Roadmap – Whether You List or Not

Finally, we'll help you map a 3-year journey to readiness.

You'll discover:

- SME IPO eligibility benchmarks (NSE Emerge, BSE SME)
- Typical timelines and partners involved
- Cost structures and preparation phases
- Alternate capital options (private equity, debt, strategic partners)
- And how to use "IPO-readiness" as a **business credibility tool** — even if you decide not to list

Because the journey of readiness itself **builds a business that's respected — listed or not.**

__Readers can attend our SME IPO Webinars to learn about__ SME IPO eligibility benchmarks (NSE Emerge, BSE SME).

This Chapter Is About Taking Yourself Seriously — Before Others Do

☑ You've built a real business.

☑ Now it's time to build a **credible company.**

☑ One that stands up to questions earns respect and **inspires belief.**

Let's get ready. Let's scale with structure. Let's prepare to go public — even if you remain private.

You owe it to your vision, your team, and your future.

Let's begin.

What IPO Readiness Really Means:

More Than Just Financials

You've come a long way.

Your sales engine is humming.

Your systems are structured.

Your team is stabilising.

Your brand is building equity.

And your growth story is finally worth talking about.

Now comes the million-dollar question — sometimes quite literally:

"Can your business stand tall under scrutiny — from investors, banks, partners, or even the public market?"

Because at some point, every ambitious MSME reaches a turning point.

You no longer want to be just profitable.

You want to be *fundable*.

You want scale — not just stability.

You want to be seen as a **serious, structured, future-ready company.**

This is where **IPO readiness** becomes your next big shift.

IPO readiness is not about listing your company today — it's about making your business strong, transparent, and investment-worthy... even if you never go public.

This chapter will walk you through installing the discipline, systems, governance, and visibility needed to make your business **IPO-capable—even if you don't plan to list right away.**

Preparation gives you **options**—to raise capital, attract premium clients, earn supplier trust, or even invite strategic investors.

The Problem: Most MSMEs Misunderstand IPO as a Financial Event

Ask a room full of SME founders, "What do you think IPO readiness means?" and you'll hear:

- "We're too small. IPO is still far away."
- "IPO is only for large businesses."
- "My CA says we'll consider it once we cross ₹100 crore."
- "It's too complex — I don't understand the process."

These beliefs are limiting — and incorrect.

While revenue and profitability are important, they are just **part** of the picture.

What really matters to regulators, investors, and the stock exchange is:

Can your business survive scrutiny and scale without the founder being involved in every small detail?

That's the true meaning of being IPO-ready.

The Agitation: Waiting for Size Before Preparing = Missed Opportunity

Let's look at what happens when you delay readiness:

- You suddenly get a funding opportunity — but can't produce clean MIS or audited numbers
- A merchant banker shows interest — but you don't have board minutes, compliance trails, or cost reports
- A strategic investor wants to visit — but your HR, IT, and vendor contracts are informal
- You want to apply for a government scheme — but your financial documentation is patchy
- You plan to scale — but your internal team isn't ready for structured growth

You're caught off guard. Not because your business is weak — but because your **systems are invisible.**

And in the world of capital and compliance, **invisibility equals risk.**

The Solution: Think of IPO Readiness as a Business Operating System

Let's shift your mindset.

IPO readiness doesn't start with a merchant banker.

It starts with the **founder deciding** to run their business with:

- Financial discipline
- Transparent documentation
- Defined roles and responsibilities
- Governance and reporting systems
- Long-term strategic clarity

It's about building a company that:

☑ Can raise money

☑ Can expand into new geographies

☑ Can attract top talent

☑ Can survive a founder's absence

☑ Can scale — with or without you

That's the heart of IPO readiness.

The 6 Pillars of True IPO Readiness

Most MSMEs think that if they make an impressive balance sheet (even if manipulated), they will be able to float an IPO. The market is right now flooded with some fake advisors who misguide the gullible MSME promoters. Tax avoidance another big reason which keeps the MSMEs deprived of the IPO opportunity. Let's break down what it really means to be IPO-ready — beyond the balance sheet:

Pillar	Why It Matters
1. **Clean Financials**	Investors don't back guesses. They back numbers.
2. **Founder Independence**	No one wants to fund a one-person dependency.
3. **Operational Systems**	Scale breaks without standardisation.
4. **Board & Governance**	You need a structure that allows for accountability.
5. **Growth Story Clarity**	People fund potential — if it's well articulated.
6. **Legal & Statutory Hygiene**	Non-compliance kills deals, regardless of profit.

These are the new checkboxes for credibility — not just compliance.

Real-World Example: Two ₹50 Crore Companies — One Gets Funded, One Doesn't

Let's compare:

Company A	Company B
₹50 Cr revenue	₹48 Cr revenue
Founder does all pricing & hiring	A team of 4 leaders with roles defined
No documented SOPs	Processes documented & followed
CA closes books once a year	Monthly MIS with CFO review
Zero board governance	The advisory board meets quarterly
GST and PF delays	Clean compliance calendar
No clear vision	3-year scale roadmap + unit economics

Which company gets a better valuation?

Which one clears due diligence faster?

Which one will be ready for SME IPO?

The answer is obvious.

The Key Belief Shift: From Growth-Driven to Structure-Led

You've hustled, innovated, and pushed your MSME to a respectable level.

Now, it's time to evolve.

From founder-run → system-run

From relationship-driven → data-driven

From cash mindset → reporting mindset

From survival business → strategic business

Even if you never list your company, **preparing for an IPO will elevate your business's perception and performance.**

Quick Self-Check: Are You IPO-Ready (or Getting There)?

☑ Do you get a full MIS report by the 10th of every month?

☑ Is there a system for approvals, reporting, and compliance — not just memory?

☑ Do you properly document SOPs, board decisions, and team roles?

☑ Can your business run for 10 days without you — without collapsing?

☑ Do you have a 2–3-year vision to excite a banker, investor, or advisor?

If not, don't wait for a merchant banker to tell you.

Start building the structure today.

Because readiness is **not about listing.**

It's about building a business that can — if you choose.

Clean Up Operations, Governance & Reporting:

When a small business grows, it often runs on hustle, memory, and the founder's judgment. Decisions are made on the fly. Processes are fluid. Compliance is often reactive. This flexibility may serve you initially, but it becomes a liability the moment your business needs to scale, attract capital, or pass through scrutiny.

"You can't prepare for investment or IPO with shortcuts. You need structure."

The market doesn't just reward profitable companies. It rewards transparent, well-governed, and operationally disciplined companies.

In this chapter, we'll show you how to clean up your operations, governance, and reporting systems so that your business looks stable from the outside and becomes investor-ready from within.

The Problem: MSMEs Often Grow Without Structure

Many MSMEs operate fast, functionally, and informally. Documents are stored in emails or scattered folders. Approvals are verbal. Key knowledge lives inside one or two team members' heads. The owner is the final authority on everything—from pricing to hiring to payments.

This informality works when the scale is small. But it creates chaos as the business grows.

Without structured operations:

- You lose time in repetitive tasks
- You can't train new hires efficiently
- Client experience becomes inconsistent
- Vendors complain about delays and miscommunication
- You struggle to track performance across departments

Most importantly, your business will begin to look **risky** to outsiders.

No investor or strategic partner will engage with a company where basic hygiene is lacking. They may not say it directly, but the due diligence process will.

The Agitation: Lack of Governance = Lost Credibility

Let's consider what happens when governance and reporting are weak:

- A government scheme requires board resolutions — you have none documented
- A potential investor requests monthly MIS — you don't even have standard reports
- An auditor asks for compliance logs — your CA scrambles to recreate history
- A bank seeks vendor agreements and SOPs — you realise they don't exist formally
- Your leadership team wants clarity on decision rights — but roles were never defined

What was once seen as flexibility now becomes a red flag.

"If your business doesn't run on systems, it runs on risk."

You may have real profits, loyal clients, and a good team. But poor documentation, zero governance, and inconsistent reporting make your business look immature — even if it's high-performing.

The Solution: Formalise Without Overcomplicating

You don't have to become a corporate overnight.

You must bring **clarity, structure, and traceability** into your business's operations.

Let's break it down into three areas:

1. Operational Clean-Up – From Memory to System

Start by identifying the top 10–15 recurring processes in your business. These could be:

- Sales enquiry handling
- , Quotation approval
- , Invoicing and dispatch
- , Vendor onboarding
- , Inventory reconciliation
- , Client feedback and complaint resolution
- , Hiring and onboarding

- and Monthly review meetings.

Document these as **Standard Operating Procedures (SOPs)** — using simple tools like Word, Google Docs, or Notion.

Each SOP should cover:

- Purpose of the process
- Who is responsible?
- Step-by-step workflow
- Timelines
- Tools or templates required

This single step — SOP documentation — drastically improves onboarding, accountability, and delegation.

2. Governance Structure – From Verbal to Visible

Good governance isn't about red tape. It's about **clarity and control.**

Start with the basics:

Governance Element	Why It Matters
Board or Advisory Meetings	Strategic alignment, external accountability
Documented Resolutions	Legal proof of decisions made
Founder Roles & Responsibilities	Reduces dependency and confusion
Delegation Matrix	Who approves what — and at what level
Organisational Chart	Clarifies reporting lines and communication flow

If you're not ready for a full-fledged board, form an **advisory panel** — 2–3 experienced professionals or mentors who meet quarterly to review your business and guide decisions.

Their presence itself improves how seriously others take your company.

3. Reporting Discipline – From Gut Feeling to Data-Driven

Every serious business needs regular, standardised reporting. This includes:

- **Monthly MIS** (Management Information System): Revenue, expenses, profit, outstanding receivables, vendor dues
- **Weekly dashboards**: Sales pipeline, lead conversion, fulfilment status
- **Department-wise KPIs**: Marketing, sales, operations, finance, HR
- **Compliance checklist**: GST filings, TDS, PF/ESIC, ROC, audit timelines

To automate as much as possible, use tools like Google Sheets, Tally, Zoho Books, or custom dashboards. Share reports with relevant team members and review them in monthly internal meetings.

When data flows regularly, decisions become faster and smarter. In just 3–6 months, your business goes from **chaotic to credible**.

Quick Self-Check: Are You Operationally and Governance-Ready?

☑ Are at least 10 core processes documented with SOPs?

☑ Do you conduct quarterly review meetings (internal or external)?

☑ Are your approval systems written down and followed?

☑ Do you have a clean digital trail of decisions and filings?

☑ Are MIS and KPI dashboards shared consistently with your team?

If not, begin with a one-week "Clean-Up Sprint" — gather your team, list current gaps, assign owners, and start the transformation.

Because readiness is not a project; it's a **culture of structure.**

Build a Financial & Compliance Culture:

Think Like a CFO, Not Just a Founder

A business can grow without financial discipline.

But it cannot scale or sustain without it.

"Sales bring in revenue. But structure protects it."

Many MSME founders are extremely good at what they do — marketing, selling, managing operations — but finance is often treated as an afterthought or handed over entirely to the accountant.

This may work for a while.

Until one day, you realise:

- You have revenue... but don't know your true profit
- You have bank balance... but no clarity on cash flow
- You have clients... but don't know your receivables
- You have multiple GST registrations... but inconsistent filings
- You have a growing team... but no cost-centre tracking

This chapter is about changing that reality.

It's time to shift from a "CA-only" approach to a **culture where financial clarity becomes everyone's responsibility** — from founder to team leads to back-office staff.

The Problem: Founders Stay Blind to the Numbers

Most MSME owners rely heavily on their accountant or CA for everything financial.

They call once a month (or quarter), ask a few basic questions, and move on. In some cases, they only focus on tax saving — not decision-making.

The result?

- No monthly financial reviews
- No standard ratio tracking
- No budgeting or forecasting
- No cost analysis per project, product, or client
- No dashboard to see how the business is truly performing

This is dangerous.

Because when you operate without data, you make decisions based on gut feeling — not facts.

And in a competitive, regulated world — the gut is not good enough.

The Agitation: Poor Financial Hygiene Destroys Trust & Value

Imagine this scenario:

An investor is interested in your company. You're confident and walk into the meeting with passion.

But when they ask:

- "What was your gross margin last quarter?"
- "How does your revenue split across products or locations?"
- "What's your working capital cycle?"
- "Can I see your last 6 months' MIS and P&L?"
- "What are your top 5 expense heads and their monthly trend?"

You pause. Or you fumble. Or worse — you say, "Let me check with my CA."

You may still be profitable.

But to them — **you're not in control**.

"Investors don't just want good numbers. They want founders who know those numbers — cold."

The Solution: Build a Finance-First Operating Rhythm

Financial control isn't about being a finance expert.

It's about having a **structured rhythm** to track, review, and act on your business numbers.

Let's now walk through the practical steps to build that rhythm into your MSME.

Step 1: Establish a Monthly MIS Review

Every month — ideally by the 7th or 10th — you should receive a standardised **Management Information System (MIS)** report. This can be built in Excel, Google Sheets, or tools like Zoho Books, Tally, or QuickBooks.

The MIS must contain at least the following:

Report Component	What It Tells You
Profit & Loss Statement	Revenue, gross margin, net profit
Balance Sheet Snapshot	Assets, liabilities, equity
Cash Flow Summary	Inflows, outflows, net cash position
Receivables Aging	Outstanding collections and delays
Payables Summary	Vendor dues and upcoming payments
Expense Trend Report	Top 5–10 recurring expenses and variances

Make it a monthly ritual. Review with your internal team — not just your accountant.

Step 2: Track Financial Ratios That Actually Matter

Don't just look at revenue. Start tracking 5–6 key financial ratios that give insight into your business health:

Ratio	Ideal Purpose
Gross Profit Margin (%)	Are you pricing and sourcing right?
Net Profit Margin (%)	Are operations and overheads controlled?
Working Capital Cycle (days)	How fast do you convert input to cash?
Debtor Days	How long does it take to collect payment?
Operating Expense Ratio	Are costs rising faster than revenue?
Return on Capital Employed	Are you using funds effectively?

Add these ratios to your MIS every month. Review the trend — not just the numbers.

Step 3: Create Cost Centres & Budget Ownership

As your business grows, so does complexity.

You need to know:

- Which product lines or projects are profitable
- Which branches or departments are leaking cash
- Where your team is overspending — and where they're saving

To enable this, build **cost centres** in your accounting system:

Cost Centre Type	Examples
Product/Service Line	Website design, packaging, fabrication
Business Unit/Location	Jaipur office, Plant 1, Online sales
Department/Function	HR, Sales, Marketing, R&D

Assign budgets to each. Review actual vs. planned spending monthly. Let your team own their numbers. This builds **accountability and awareness.**

Step 4: Automate Compliance Tracking

Many MSMEs struggle with:

- Missed GST deadlines
- Incorrect TDS filings
- Late ROC submissions
- Statutory audit delays
- Employee PF/ESI mismatches

This erodes credibility fast.

Create a **compliance calendar** — and assign clear ownership:

Compliance Type	Frequency	Responsible Person
GST Filing	Monthly	Accounts Manager
TDS Payment	Monthly	Accountant
ROC Filing	Annually	Company Secretary
PF/ESI Filing	Monthly	HR or Payroll Specialist
Annual Audit	Annually	CA + Internal Coordinator

Use tools like Google Calendar, Trello, or WhatsApp reminders to stay ahead. A compliant business is not just legal — it's **investable.**

Real-World Snapshot: Before vs After Financial Discipline

Parameter	Before	After
Revenue Review	Only at year-end	Monthly with team-level breakdown
Profitability Awareness	Founder's guess	Accurate P&L with project margin tracking
Cash Flow	Manual monitoring	Automated cash flow dashboard
Compliance	Last-minute chaos	Calendar-based, pre-planned filing
Team Financial Awareness	Zero	Managers know cost, budget, variance

You go from **reactive to reliable**, which changes how banks, partners, and investors see you.

Quick Self-Check: Are You Running with Financial Clarity?

☑ Do you receive and review an MIS every month?

☑ Can you answer margin, cash, and debt questions confidently?

☑ Do you know your debtor days and working capital cycle?

☑ Is your compliance calendar structured and maintained?

☑ Are your teams aware of their cost and budget numbers?

If not, block two hours to set up your basic finance review process this week.

You don't need a CFO.

You just need to **think like one — consistently.**

Leadership, Board, & Systems:

That Impress Investors

Most MSMEs are built around a strong founder.

But the ones that scale — and get investor attention — are built around a strong **system**.

"Founders build businesses. Systems build companies."

In the previous section, we focused on financial and compliance discipline.

Now, we go one step further.

Even if your numbers are impressive, serious investors, lenders, and strategic partners will ask a deeper question:

"Can this business run — grow — and evolve without being dependent on just one person?"

That's where leadership systems, governance, and structured decision-making come in.

In this chapter, you'll learn how to build that internal credibility — not just for IPO readiness but to become the kind of company the market respects and follows.

The Problem: Most MSMEs Are Founder-Dependent — Not Founder-Led

The typical MSME structure looks like this:

- The founder is the central brain
- Every key decision passes through them
- Approvals, hiring, pricing, vendor changes — all require their input
- There are managers — but they're executors, not owners
- There's no second line of leadership
- And the board — if it exists at all — is passive or symbolic

This structure may work till ₹20–30 crore. But it starts breaking beyond that.

Because:

- You cannot be everywhere
- You cannot think of everything
- And you certainly cannot scale everything

"What gets investors excited is not just your vision — but your ability to delegate, scale, and lead through others."

The Agitation: Lack of Leadership Systems = No Scalability, No Valuation

Even profitable businesses hit a glass ceiling when:

- They can't develop a second line of leadership
- Founders micromanage instead of empowering
- Decision-making is slow or unclear
- There's no formal board or governance process
- No succession plan is in place
- The business runs on habit, not structure

Investors know this.

They don't just see risk in numbers. They see risk in people dependency.

"If your team cannot run the business without you — your business is not scalable; it's survivable."

The Solution: Build Leadership & Governance That Inspire Confidence

You don't need an MBA-style leadership model. You need to:

✔ Formalise your leadership structure

✔ Bring external accountability

✔ Establish rhythm-based decision-making

✔ Empower people with clarity

✔ And signal seriousness to outsiders

Let's break this into five parts:

1. Create a Simple Leadership Framework

Start with a visual **Organisational Structure**. Define 4–6 key functions in your business:

Function	Examples
Sales	Lead generation, closures, targets
Operations	Fulfilment, dispatch, quality
Finance	Accounting, MIS, cash flow
HR & Admin	Hiring, training, compliance
Marketing	Branding, content, lead pipeline
Strategy	New initiatives, partnerships

Assign a leader (or interim owner) for each — even if it's yourself initially.

Clarify responsibilities. Set KPIs. Review progress monthly.

This creates **role clarity** and begins the journey from "me" to "we".

2. Appoint Advisors or a Working Board

Even if you're not legally required to have a board, form an **advisory council**.

This could be:

- A retired industry veteran
- A CA or CFO with governance experience

- A mentor who understands the scale
- A lawyer or compliance expert
- A peer entrepreneur you trust

Hold a **quarterly board meeting**. Share performance updates. Ask for input. Take notes and follow-up actions.

This brings **external accountability and strategic direction**.

And it gives your investors' confidence that you're not building in isolation.

3. Document Decision Rights & Delegation

Most MSME teams operate in a grey zone:

- "Should I approve this?"
- "Can I offer a 5% discount?"
- "Who's allowed to change vendor terms?"
- "Is this a founder-level call?"

Document a **Delegation of Authority Matrix (DoA)** — a simple table outlining:

Decision Type	Who Can Decide
Pricing below 5% margin	Sales Head with Finance approval
Hiring up to ₹25K/month	HR Manager
Vendor onboarding	Operations Head + Finance review
Capital expenditure >₹1L	Founder + Board input

This reduces back-and-forth and builds **empowered execution**.

4. Install a Leadership Rhythm

Great companies don't just meet when there's a problem.

They run on **structured leadership rhythms.**

Adopt this simple model:

Meeting Type	Frequency	Focus Area
Daily Huddle	Daily	Team updates, blockers, priorities
Weekly Leadership	Weekly	KPIs, cross-functional review
Monthly Strategy	Monthly	Big picture, plans, pivots
Quarterly Board	Quarterly	Governance, growth, guidance

Use dashboards, trackers, and agendas to keep these productive.

5. Prepare a Succession & Transition Plan

One of the biggest risks in founder-led MSMEs is:

"What happens if the founder falls sick, retires, or exits?"

Create a **succession folder** that contains the following:

- Key contacts and relationships
- Access to accounts, systems, and dashboards
- Status of ongoing projects

- Roles and responsibilities of key people
- Legal and statutory obligations
- Your vision for the next 3–5 years

Share this with your board or core team.

This isn't about stepping away. It's about building resilience.

Real-World Snapshot: Before vs After Leadership Systemisation

Area	Before	After
Decision-making	Centralised with founder	Delegated with clarity
Team ownership	Task-driven	KPI-driven leaders
Strategic input	Internal only	External advisors with perspective
Meetings	Ad hoc, reactive	Structured with agendas
Succession	No plan	The basic playbook in place

This doesn't just improve operations — it **elevates perception.**

Quick Self-Check: Are You Systemising Leadership?

☑ Do you have an updated org chart with clear function owners?

☑ Have you appointed at least one external advisor or mentor?

☑ Do your team members know what decisions they can make?

☑ Are leadership meetings regular, structured, and data-backed?

☑ Is there a basic succession file or emergency continuity plan?

If not — start with two simple steps:

1. Draft your org chart and discuss it with your leadership team.
2. Identify one mentor who can guide you as a board advisor.

Build not just a team — build a **leadership ecosystem.**

Create Your IPO Roadmap:

Whether You List or Not

You've established the financial discipline, governance structure, operational systems, and leadership mechanisms, transforming a business from founder-driven to investor-ready.

The next question is:

"How do I know if — and when — I'm ready to go public?"

But here's a better question:

"Even if I don't list now, can I prepare in a way that keeps the door open — strategically, structurally, and systematically?"

This is what the IPO roadmap is all about.

It's not just about filing a DRHP or ringing the bell at the stock exchange.

It's about running your MSME in a way that builds **transparency, trust, and scalability** — so that if and when the opportunity comes, you're ready. And even if it doesn't, you've still built a company that earns respect, attracts capital, and operates at a higher level of maturity.

The Problem: IPO is Treated Like a Distant Dream

Most founders think of IPO as something that's:

- Too far
- Too complex
- Too expensive
- For unicorns or corporates, only
- Only for businesses doing ₹100–200 crore and above

But that's outdated thinking.

In India, the rise of **SME IPO platforms** (like NSE Emerge and BSE SME) has opened the door for companies with as little as ₹10 crore post-issue capital, ₹1.5–2 crore profitability, and a track record of just 3 years.

And yet, most MSMEs never prepare — not because they're unfit, but because they're **uninformed**.

The Agitation: When You Don't Prepare, You Miss the Window

The real cost of not preparing is not "no IPO".

It's that you:

- Can't raise capital when needed
- Lose investor interest due to structural gaps
- Miss government or institutional incentives
- Can't exit or dilute stake strategically
- Struggle to justify valuation beyond revenue multiples
- Remain invisible in your market — despite strong performance

The worst part? These opportunities don't knock twice.

Without readiness, your business might survive. But it won't **scale with peace and power**.

The Solution: Build a Visual, Practical IPO Readiness Roadmap

Let's now map out a step-by-step IPO readiness plan that MSMEs can follow — whether you intend to list or want to build as you could.

Step 1: Understand SME IPO Eligibility (India)

For most small and mid-sized businesses, the SME platforms of NSE and BSE are more accessible than mainboard listings. The eligibility criteria keeps on changing. Readers are advised to visit the website of NSE Emerge or BSE SME for latest requirements. To understand the eligibility criteria and other relevant information, you can attend our SME IPO Webinar https://bmaggarwal.com/sme-ipo

You don't need to meet all the criteria today.

But now you know **what to aim for**.

Step 2: Build a 3-Year IPO Readiness Timeline

Here's a simple model:

Year	Focus Area	Key Actions
Year 1	Structure & Clean-Up	SOPs, MIS, dashboards, governance, compliance
Year 2	Financial Strength & Visibility	Consistent profitability, cost control, margin tracking
Year 3	External Alignment & Strategy	Advisors, valuation prep, DRHP consultants, merchant banker

Create a shared roadmap document. Review it quarterly.

Step 3: Identify Gaps Using a Readiness Scorecard

Build a simple scorecard that helps you rate your readiness:

Area	Score (0–5)	Comment/Action Required
Financial Reporting Quality		
Compliance Calendar		
MIS Discipline		
Leadership Delegation		
SOP & Documentation		
Client/Revenue Concentration		
Gross & Net Margins		
Board/Advisory Engagement		
Brand Positioning		

This gives you a snapshot of where you stand — and where to improve.

Step 4: Appoint IPO Readiness Partners

You don't need to walk this path alone.

Start identifying:

- A CA or CFO who has handled IPO filings or due diligence
- A legal advisor for ROC, shareholder agreements, and compliance
- A merchant banker (for actual listing — later stage)
- A brand and communication consultant for positioning
- Internal champions — someone from your own team who can manage IPO documentation and timelines

Create a "Readiness Circle" — 4–5 people who guide and challenge you.

Step 5: Use IPO Readiness as a Credibility Tool: Even if You Don't List

Here's the final mindset shift:

IPO readiness is not a goal. It's a reputation framework.

When you prepare with this level of seriousness, the world responds accordingly:

- Banks give better terms
- Partners trust your governance
- Investors look at you seriously
- Clients treat you with higher regard
- Employees feel part of a larger vision

This is not a theory. It's what serious MSMEs across India are already doing — quietly preparing to compete at the highest level.

Real-World Snapshot: IPO vs IPO-Ready vs Informal

Attribute	Informal Business	IPO-Ready Business	Listed Business
Governance	Founder-driven	System & board-led	SEBI-compliant
Reporting	On request	Monthly, structured	Mandatory disclosures
Valuation Understanding	Absent	Industry benchmarked	Market-determined
Investor Conversation	Not happening	Ongoing	Active
Talent Attraction	Hard	Better	High

Becoming IPO-ready shifts you one level higher — permanently.

Quick Self-Check: Are You IPO-Ready in Principle?

☑ Have you mapped out your next 3-year IPO readiness plan?

☑ Do you know your current eligibility on NSE/BSE SME benchmarks?

☑ Are you tracking monthly financials and governance updates?

☑ Do you have at least one external advisor guiding your readiness?

☑ Can you explain your business story, metrics, and vision?

If not, block a weekend.

Create your roadmap.

Present it to your leadership team.

Review it every quarter.

You may not go public next year — but when the opportunity comes, you won't be starting from scratch.

You'll be starting **from strength.**

What You've Just Built...

With this final section, your MSME has now transformed from a hardworking business to a **high-potential, structured, scalable company**.

You've:

- Cleaned your systems
- Clarified your numbers

- Delegated with purpose
- Installed governance
- And now, define your pathway to public or partner-ready credibility

Congratulations.

You're not just running a business.

You're building a legacy.

What's Next on Your Smart MSME Journey?

Congratulations!
You've done something most business owners never do — you've invested time to understand not just how to grow, but how to **grow smartly**.

You've walked through the entire Smart MSME Blueprint: From fixing leaks in your sales engine to positioning your brand to stand out... From building team systems to preparing for institutional readiness...
From chaos to clarity... and now, from **founder-led effort to scalable enterprise**.

But here's the truth:
Books open your mind. But action transforms your business.

So, what should you do next?

◆ 1. Join Our Monthly SME IPO Webinars

If the idea of going public feels exciting — or intimidating — start by attending our **free monthly SME IPO awareness webinar**.
These sessions break down:

- Why more Indian SMEs are choosing the IPO route
- What criteria really matter

- How valuation, funding, and compliance can be turned into growth drivers
- And how you can assess your own IPO readiness — even if you're not "big enough" yet

🎯 **To register**, visit: https://bmaggarwal.com/sme-ipo/

◈ 2. Enrol in the Smart MSME Course (Coming Soon)

We're building something special — a **live and recorded video course** based entirely on the systems, frameworks, and tools you read in this book.

This will include:

- Practical walkthroughs of business dashboards
- Offer & positioning exercises
- Sales machine systems
- Live Q&A sessions
- SME IPO readiness checklist
- Templates, tools, trackers — all ready for implementation

📋 Want early access? Join the waitlist now at: www.bmaggarwal.com/course

◈ 3. Stay Connected — Join the MSME Growth Circle

You don't have to do this alone. The MSME Growth Circle is India's most trusted mentorship ecosystem for serious founders ready to build, scale, and step up.

Inside, you'll find:

- Community of like-minded MSME founders
- Live sessions, implementation challenges, tools, and accountability
- Founder-focused insights — with no jargon, no fluff

📬 Join the community: www.bmaggarwal.com/join

Final Words

You don't have to stay stuck.
You don't have to scale alone.
And you certainly don't have to do it the hard way.

You now have the roadmap. Let's walk it together — with systems, strategy, and support.

The best time to scale smart was 3 years ago. The next best time is today.

See you inside the Growth Circle.

CA B. M. Aggarwal
Chartered Accountant | MSME Mentor | IPO Strategist
Founder – MSME Growth Circle
www.bmaggarwal.com

📚 FROM THE SAME AUTHOR

📖 **The Smart MSME: Scale Smart. Get IPO Ready**
A full-scale growth blueprint — from eliminating chaos to creating a systemised, scalable, and IPO-ready business.
👉 *You're reading it now.*

📖 **Indian SMEs & The Power of SME IPO**
A practical and founder-friendly playbook for preparing, planning, and executing a successful SME IPO under Indian regulations.
🔗 Available on Amazon
https://amzn.to/3KN6JK4

📖 **Pitch Like a Pro**
Master the fundraising journey — from pitch decks and investor objections to crafting your valuation narrative. Perfect for startups and SMEs alike.
🔗 Available on Amazon
https://www.amazon.in/dp/B0F9VKSX2V

Appendix: Tools & Resources

Below are the curated tools, templates, and platforms referenced throughout this book. These are the same resources we use and recommend to MSMEs looking to scale smartly and prepare for IPO readiness.

Please visit www.bmaggarwal.com/tools

Business Systems & Automation

- **New Zenler:** Our recommended platform for building and delivering online courses and trainings.
- **WaSender:** Tool for automating WhatsApp follow-ups, reminders, and lead communication.
- **TeleCRM:** CRM designed for Indian businesses with built-in calling, lead pipelines, and follow-up tracking.

Lead Generation & Sales

- **Canva:** Design tools for banners, pitch decks, social posts, and landing pages.
- **Google Forms / Typeform:** Used for lead capture, surveys, and application workflows.
- **Calendly:** For scheduling discovery or consultation calls with automation.

IPO Readiness & Business Clarity

- **Smart MSME Diagnostic Tool:** Download your free scorecard at: www.bmaggarwal.com/resources
- **Weekly Pulse Dashboard:** Track performance weekly across departments.

• **Sales Leak Tracker:** Spot and plug the 5 invisible sales leaks in your system.

• **Smart Offer Canvas:** Craft and compare high-conversion product/service offers.

Support & Learning

• **Join Our Free MSME IPO Webinar:** Learn about SME IPO eligibility, benefits, and next steps: www.bmaggarwal.com/sme-ipo

• **The MSME Growth Circle:** Get access to our founder community, live sessions, and business-building tools.

Disclosure: Some of the tools above may include affiliate links. We only recommend tools we trust and use ourselves.